BRITISH INTERNAL USERS

by

Roger Butcher

Published by:-
South Coast Transport Publishing
Hampshire, England

ISBN 1 872768 09 1

CONTENTS

Abbreviations	2
Introduction	3
London Midland Region	
Current Stock	5
Vehicles No Longer In Stock	11
Eastern Region	
Current Stock	32
Vehicles No Longer In Stock	42
Western Region	
Current Stock	65
Vehicles No Longer In Stock	68
Southern Region	
Current Stock	80
Vehicles No Longer In Stock	82
Scottish Region	
Current Stock	91
Vehicles No Longer In Stock	92

ABBREVIATIONS

The following abbreviations are used in this publication:-

BREL	British Rail Engineering Limited
BRML	British Rail Maintenance Limited
CAD	Central Ammunition Depot
CARMD	Carriage Maintenance Depot
CE	Civil Engineers
CED	Combined Engineering Depot
CMD	Central Materials Depot
CS	Carriage Sidings
CWMD	Carriage and Wagon Maintenance Depot
ECD	Electrification Construction Depot
ECJS	East Coast Joint Stock
EMU	Electric Multiple Unit
EY	Engineers Yard
FD	Freight Depot
FLT	Freightliner Terminal
FP	Fuelling Point
GER	Great Eastern Railway
LIFT	London International Freight Terminal
LIP	Locomotive Inspection Point
LT	London Transport
MoD	Ministry of Defence
MoDAD	Ministry of Defence Army Department
OHLM	Overhead Line Maintenance
OTPD	On-Track Plant Depot
PAD	Pre-Assembley Depot
PW	Permanent Way
RCE	Regional Civil Engineers
RNAD	Royal Naval Armament Depot
RTC	Railway Technical Centre
SD	Servicing Depot
S&T	Signal & Telecommunications
TMD	Traction Maintenance Depot
T&RSMD	Traction and Rolling Stock Maintenance Depot
WRD	Wagon Repair Depot

INTRODUCTION

The principle aim of this book is simply to detail accurately what internal user vehicles British Railways possesses, to give their former identity and type and to state where each vehicle can be found. Such a list has not been available before and this book has therefore been published in order to meet the demand for such a list.

The very name "internal user" indicates quite clearly that it refers to vehicles which are not supposed to travel on running lines but are confined to yards and depots. Within this category are many wagons but also a significant of coaches and vans appropriated from either capital or departmental coaching stock. Although the allocated location is normally static it is by no means unknown for internal users to be transferred from one location to another, special permission having to be obtained before movement can be made.

Each region is split into "Current Stock" and "Vehicles No Longer In Stock", the latter section giving a brief history of every number allocated since 1980 but for which the vehicle is now either scrapped, resold or preserved. Full information is also given in this section on cancelled numbers. This historical content reflects the upsurge in interest in the BR internal user fleet since the early 1980s, although the specific allocation dates of 024400, 041500, 060900 and 083400 are actually 3/80, 3/80, 10/79 and 10/80 respectively. However it was felt more appropriate to start each historical section at the beginning of a block of one hundred numbers. As the Scottish Region has had relatively few internal users all known historical information is included.

Mention needs to be made that since 6th April 1992 BR now operates a business-led organisation, but that until 1st January 1993 or 1st April 1993 the traditional internal user numbering series will continue. Thus all internal users located in Scotland, of whatever business, will continue to be allocated a number in the 09XXXX series.

It should be clearly stated that those readers requiring either more detailed information on vehicle types or information such as diagrams, lot numbers, measurements etc should cross reference the former identity listed with the various books written by wagon experts with the modeller or railway historian in mind.

Basically as regards the three letter carkind, the first letter indicates the wagon or type group and often this is derived from the type of wagon i.e. Group F for flat wagons. The second letter of the code identifies the actual type or fleet within the group and this may be by weight, size, duty or another distinguishing factor. The final letter indicates the brake type fitted. Briefly those relevant to this publication can be summarised as follows:-

Main Type

B	Bogie Steel Carrying
CA	Brake Vans (Traffic Department)
F	Flat Wagons
H	Hoppers
M	Mineral Wagons
O	Open Wagons
P	Privately Owned Wagons
R	Railway Operating Vehicles
Q	Departmental Coaching Stock Vehicles
S	Steel Carrying - 2 Axle
T	Tank Wagons - Privately Owned
V	Vans

```
X    Exceptional Vehicles and Special Purpose Vehicles
Y    Departmental Bogie Freight Vehicles
Z    Departmental Stock - 2 Axle Freight Vehicles
```

<u>Brake Type</u>

```
A    Air Brake
B    Air Brake, through vacuum pipe
O    No power brake
Q    No power brake, through air pipe
R    Unfitted with through air and vacuum pipes
V    Vacuum brake
W    Vacuum brake, through air pipe
X    Dual brake (air and vacuum)
```

As regards internal users now owned by private companies the few remaining vehicles owned by Associated British Ports are not included. However those internal users still surviving on BREL premises have been included as many of them have been allocated internal user numbers during the 1980s.

As mentioned above the numbering of internal user vehicles is on a regional basis and further notes on each number series will be found at the beginning of the relevant section. It needs to be emphasised that this book reflects vehicles that have been allocated internal user numbers and does not include vehicles in unofficial internal use. In addition an asterisk indicates those vehicles which do not yet carry their allocated internal user number.

This first edition has been prepared to reflect the very latest situation and incorporates all information known to me on 1st September 1992.

Finally, I would like to record my thanks to the many railway staff from all points of British Railways who have for many years been regularly assisting me in my efforts to maintain an accurate and comprehensive register of BR Internal User Vehicles. Thanks as always to Keith, Mike, Roger, Brian and the KBTCB for their help and also the photographers for supplying the photographs included. My thanks also to Diane and Mark whose continuing support and encouragement has been greatly appreciated.

Roger Butcher
September 1992

LONDON MIDLAND REGION – 02XXXX

Allocated numbers have reached 025005. Vehicles numbered up to 024800 should have their number engraved on a plate attached to the frame. The number series began in July 1950 with 020000 and has been used consecutively ever since.

Current Stock

No.	Former Identity	Carkind	Location
021407	Trolley 723	-	BREL Crewe
022285	ESSO1565	TRO	Saltley LIP
023204 *	DM284255	ZRO	Machynlleth FP
023215 *	DM62	ZRO	Machynlleth FP
023657	E141383	VVO	Shrewsbury Station Sidings
024177 *	B214083	MCO	BREL Derby Litchurch Lane
024178	B184872	MCO	BREL Derby Litchurch Lane
024179	B22454	MCO	BREL Derby Litchurch Lane
024223	M499852	STO	BRML Wolverton
024242 *	B852310	VSV	RTC Derby
024296	A6090	TTO	RTC Derby
024303	TDW298	ZQO	Shrewsbury Station Sidings
024305	B476472	OHV	Tyseley CS and TMD
024306	B723366	OSV	Tyseley CS and TMD
024307	B724319	OSV	Tyseley CS and TMD
024310	B761253	VVV	Edge Hill CARMD
024318	DM157754	ZQO	Crewe Gresty Road FD
024319	DM175756	ZQO	Crewe Gresty Road FD
024327	DB749670	ZRO	BREL Crewe
024328	CDB749677	ZRO	BREL Crewe
024329	CDW43914	ZRO	BREL Crewe
024330	CDW43930	ZRO	BREL Crewe
024341	DE960602	YAO	Northampton CMD
024344	DE470802	YAO	Northampton CMD
024346	B945512	BCO	Northampton CMD
024349	DE301540	YAO	Northampton CMD
024352	B922366	BCO	Newton Heath CE Depot
024360	B944065	BCO	Northampton CMD
024365	B943600	BCO	Northampton CMD
024366	B944039	BCO	Northampton CMD
024372	DE544430	YAO	Northampton CMD
024379	DM395566	QRV	Crewe Gresty Road S&T Yard
024383	B775966	VVV	Bescot Yard
024389	DE217292	YAO	Northampton CMD
024391	DB994025	YAO	Northampton CMD
024392	DB994030	YAO	Northampton CMD
024393	DS57944	YLO	Northampton PAD
024394	DE301546	YAO	Northampton CMD
024399	DE544345	YAO	Northampton PAD
024405	B778449	VVV	Toton TMD - grounded SCR
024406	B786468	VVV	Toton TMD - grounded SCR
024414 *	B777284	VVV	Toton TMD - grounded
024416 *	B786042	VVV	Derby Etches Park T&RSMD - grounded
024417	M31153	NFV	BRML Wolverton
024423	ADB480325	ZXV	Bescot Yard (en route to Coopers Metals, Handsworth)
024424	B769482	VVV	Derby Etches Park T&RSMD
024429	M31338	NFV	Langley Green (en route to Coopers Metals, Handsworth)

024430	M31340	NFV	Carlisle Upperby CWMD
024434	DB490310	ZGO	Northampton PAD
024437	M31421	NFV	Carnforth OTPD
024439	B775102	VVV	Wigan Springs Branch TMD
024446	B786748	VVV	Rugby North Yard - grounded
024447	B765621	VVV	Edge Hill CARMD
024453 *	CDB459174	ZDO	BREL Crewe
024456	B771448	VVV	Stapleford and Sandiacre
024458	M94127	NPV	Crewe Gresty Road S&T Yard
024459 *	CDB506195	ZVV	BRML Wolverton
024461	B785522	VVV	Wolverhampton Steel Terminal
024463	E94474	NPV	Edge Hill CARMD
024464	M3732	TSO	BRML Wolverton
024478	ADB999012	ZRO	Machynlleth FP
024481	ADB749656	ZRQ	Buxton TMD
024482	ADB749659	ZRQ	Willesden TMD
024484	ADB767478	ZDV	Shrewsbury Coton Hill Yard
024497	W94507	NPV	Hartley House, RTC Derby
024499	B778338	VVV	Toton TMD - grounded SCR
024500	SUKO83122	TEA	Toton Training School
024501	B785734	VVV	Edge Hill CARMD
024505	B784480	VMV	Wolverhampton Wednesfield Road
024507	B932593	RRV	Machynlleth FP
024508	B479293	OHV	Euston Down CS
024509	E296379	OHV	Euston Down CS
024510	ADM40212	QRV	Longsight TMD
024511	ADM40263	QRV	Longsight TMD
024512	ADM40326	QRV	Longsight TMD
024514	DB460675	ZAO	Chester TMD
024515 *	S1897	NQV	Tyseley TMD - grounded
024516	DM514053	ZQV	Stafford Salop Sidings
024529	ADB975795	QRV	Old Oak Common CARMD
024530	DB775853	ZRV	Wembley CARMD
024531	KDM187085	ZRO	Chester Brook Sidings
024533	B783149	VWV	Edge Hill CARMD
024534	S1770	NQV	Wolverhampton Station
024535	TDB975996	NFV	Soho OHLM Depot
024536	S1834	NQV	Tyseley TMD
024537	DB935200	ZDV	Walsall Tasker Street
024543	DB935813	ZDV	Walsall Tasker Street
024546	DB936107	ZDV	Walsall Tasker Street
024548	DB936148	ZDV	Walsall Tasker Street
024553	DB936326	ZDV	Walsall Tasker Street
024562	DB935530	ZDV	Trafford Park
024570	DB935902	ZDV	Castleton CMD
024571	DB935936	ZDV	Castleton CMD
024573	DB936002	ZDV	Castleton CMD
024576	DB936109	ZDV	Trafford Park
024603 *	CDM360337	YRP	BREL Crewe
024606	M31394	NFV	Crewe Gresty Road S&T Yard
024607	M1741	RBR	Preston North Union Yard
024611	M94237	NPV	Longsight TMD
024615	B932863	SPV	Derby Etches Park T&RSMD
024617 *	B201038	MDO	BREL Crewe
024620 *	B315859	MDO	BREL Crewe
024623 *	B950884	CAP	Monmore Green Goods Depot
024635	B555426	MCV	Duddeston WRD
024655	B419144	HTV	Pensnett Coal Depot
024656	B415409	HTV	Pensnett Coal Depot
024664 *	B462791	RFQ	BREL Derby Litchurch Lane

024666	CDB909030	YRP	Toton WRD	
024669	DB991079	ZCO	Toton Training School	
024670	S1291	RFV	Longsight TMD	
024671	S1368	RFV	Longsight TMD	
024672	M94142	RFV	Longsight TMD	
024674 *	CDB502713	ZVV	BREL Derby Litchurch Lane	
024681	B462717	RFQ	Motherwell TMD	
024682	B462725	RFQ	Holyhead Station	
024683	B462792	RFQ	Motherwell TMD	
024684	B462793	RFQ	Motherwell TMD	
024688	KDM499202	ZVO	Soho OHLM Depot	
024690 *	B745013	FVV	BREL Derby Litchurch Lane	
024695 *	KDB769039	ZRV	Crewe Gresty Road S&T Yard	
024696 *	DB996019	YMO	BREL Derby Litchurch Lane	
024697 *	DB996026	YMO	BREL Derby Litchurch Lane	
024701 *	DB996062	YMO	BREL Derby Litchurch Lane	
024703 *	DB996195	YMO	BREL Derby Litchurch Lane	
024709	ADB975892	QRV	Wembley Heavy Repair Shop	
024710	ADB975893	QRV	Wembley Heavy Repair Shop	
024711	ADB975891	QRV	Wembley Heavy Repair Shop	
024712 *	DB996161	YMO	BREL Derby Litchurch Lane	
024713 *	DB996160	YMO	BREL Derby Litchurch Lane	
024714 *	DB996094	YMO	BREL Derby Litchurch Lane	
024715 *	DB996177	YMO	BREL Derby Litchurch Lane	
024716 *	DB996056	YMO	BREL Derby Litchurch Lane	
024717 *	DB996000	YMO	BREL Derby Litchurch Lane	
024720	M94442	NPV	Chester TMD	
024721	M94705	NPV	Chester TMD	
024722	B922547	BCV	British Steel, Shelton	
024723	B922568	BCV	British Steel, Shelton	
024724	B922577	BCV	British Steel, Shelton	
024725	B922725	BCV	British Steel, Shelton	
024726	B922592	BCV	British Steel, Shelton	
024727	B922730	BCV	British Steel, Shelton	
024728	B922598	BCV	British Steel, Shelton	
024729	B922607	BCV	British Steel, Shelton	
024730	B922801	BCV	British Steel, Shelton	
024731	B922804	BCV	British Steel, Shelton	
024732	B922983	BCV	British Steel, Shelton	
024733	B922928	BCV	British Steel, Shelton	
024734	B923033	BCV	British Steel, Shelton	
024735	B945792	BCV	British Steel, Shelton	
024736	B945912	BCV	British Steel, Shelton	
024737	B945929	BCV	British Steel, Shelton	
024738	B945952	BCV	British Steel, Shelton	
024739	B945975	BCV	British Steel, Shelton	
024741	DB567764	ZHV	Ditton Creosoting Depot	
024743	E80788	NAV	Chester Brook Sidings	
024744 *	TDM395498	QPV	Old Oak Common CARMD	
024747 *	ADB875649	ZXV	RTC Derby	
024752	ADB936413	ZXV	RTC Derby	
024753	93203	NKV	Crewe Gresty Lane OTPD	
024754	KDM405789	ZGO	Crewe Gresty Road S&T Yard	
024755	KDB758994	ZDV	Crewe Gresty Road S&T Yard	
024756	KDB770468	ZDV	Crewe Gresty Road S&T Yard	
024757	ADB781058	ZRV	Northampton Castle Yard	
024759	TDB933521	ZSR	CMB Aerosols, Sutton in Ashfield	
024760	TDB936121	ZSR	CMB Aerosols, Sutton in Ashfield	
024761	ADB935708	ZVV	Carnforth	
024762	ADB769678	ZDV	Toton TMD	

024765	ADB999016	ZRO	Leicester SD
024767	ADB101136	ZRO	Llandudno Junction CS
024780	DM748029	YMO	Watford Junction
024783	TDB745628	YXV	Camden CS (to be reallocated)
024784	3744	TSO	Toton Training School
024787 *	93219	NKV	Nottingham Eastcroft OTPD
024791	KDM395377	QPV	Chester Brook Sidings
024792	KDM395767	QRV	Chester Brook Sidings
024793	KDM395844	QRV	Chester Brook Sidings
024794	ADB462740	ZSQ	RTC Derby
024795	ADB749657	ZRQ	Buxton TMD
024796	ADB781133	ZRV	Longsight TMD
024797	ADB786356	ZRV	Longsight TMD
024798	ADB761561	ZDW	Buxton TMD
024799	LDM508032	ZXV	Longsight TMD
024801	ADM395945	QQW	Toton Training School
024802	ADB999033	ZXO	Toton Training School
024804	TDB764471	ZDV	Chester WRD
024805	TDB778309	ZDV	Chester WRD
024806	B922527	BCV	British Steel, Shelton
024807	B922659	BCV	British Steel, Shelton
024808	B922693	BCV	British Steel, Shelton
024809	B922701	BCV	British Steel, Shelton
024810	B922724	BCV	British Steel, Shelton
024811	B922854	BCV	British Steel, Shelton
024812	B922908	BCV	British Steel, Shelton
024813	B922942	BCV	British Steel, Shelton
024814	B923077	BCV	British Steel, Shelton
024815	B945869	BCV	British Steel, Shelton
024816	B945893	BCV	British Steel, Shelton
024817	B945901	BCV	British Steel, Shelton
024818 *	KDB851856	ZRV	Bletchley TMD (carries 083623 in error)
024820 *	80752	NAV	Blackpool CARMD
024821 *	93594	NKV	Blackpool CARMD
024822	RDB975956	QXV	Hartley House, RTC Derby
024823 *	93483	NKV	Oxley CARMD - grounded
024824	94919	NPV	Chester WRD
024825	94335	NPV	Chester WRD
024826 *	DM163544	ZQV	Bangor Freight Yard
024827	DB920367	ZNV	Castleton CMD
024828	DB920020	ZNV	Castleton CMD
024829	DB935270	ZDV	Castleton CMD
024830	DB936247	ZDV	Castleton CMD
024831	DB935367	ZDV	Castleton CMD
024832	DB935428	ZDV	Castleton CMD
024833	DM726110	ZNV	Castleton CMD
024834	DM726927	ZNV	Castleton CMD
024835	DM726471	ZNV	Castleton CMD
024836	DB936153	ZDV	Castleton CMD
024837	DB935839	ZSV	Castleton CMD
024838	DM726882	ZNV	Castleton CMD
024839	DM726584	ZNV	Castleton CMD
024840	DB920065	ZNV	Castleton CMD
024841	DB920141	ZNV	Castleton CMD
024842	DM726962	ZNV	Castleton CMD
024843	DB920076	ZNV	Castleton CMD
024844	DB920366	ZNV	Castleton CMD
024845	DM726238	ZNV	Castleton CMD
024846	DM726332	ZNV	Castleton CMD
024847	DM726260	ZNV	Castleton CMD

024848	DM726030	ZNV		Castleton CMD
024849	DB920160	ZNV		Castleton CMD
024850	DB920389	ZNV		Castleton CMD
024851	DM726014	ZNV		Castleton CMD
024852	DB920096	ZNV		Castleton CMD
024853	DM726932	ZNV		Castleton CMD
024854	DM726974	ZNV		Castleton CMD
024855	DB920219	ZNV		Castleton CMD
024856	DM726459	ZNV		Castleton CMD
024857	DM726415	ZNV		Castleton CMD
024858	DB920082	ZNV		Castleton CMD
024859	DB920227	ZNV		Castleton CMD
024860	DM726795	ZNV		Castleton CMD
024861	DM726115	ZNV		Castleton CMD
024862	DM726500	ZNV		Castleton CMD
024863	DM726556	ZNV		Castleton CMD
024864	DB920333	ZNV		Castleton CMD
024865	DB920164	ZNV		Castleton CMD
024866	DM726497	ZNV		Castleton CMD
024867	DM726756	ZNV		Castleton CMD
024868	DB920282	ZNV		Castleton CMD
024869	DM726254	ZNV		Castleton CMD
024871	TDB932434	ZSR		Carlisle London Road Yard
024872	*	84358	NCV	RTC Derby
024874	*	CDB506889	ZVV	BRML Wolverton
024875	*	CDB507397	ZVV	BRML Wolverton
024877	*	94698	NPV	Edge Hill CARMD
024878	*	CDB502276	ZVV	BRML Wolverton
024880	*	CDB504504	ZVV	BRML Wolverton
024881	*	CDB505313	ZVV	BRML Wolverton
024883	*	CDB507398	ZVV	BRML Wolverton
024884	*	CDB507437	ZVV	BRML Wolverton
024885	*	CDB507489	ZVV	BRML Wolverton
024886	*	CDB700471	ZVV	BRML Wolverton
024887	*	CDB706036	ZVV	BRML Wolverton
024888	*	CDB709313	ZVV	BRML Wolverton
024890		93913	NKV	Derby Etches Park T&RSMD
024891		KDB764941	ZDV	British Steel, Corby
024904		RDB461074	ZXV	Old Dalby
024905		RDM478649	ZXV	Old Dalby
024906	*	RDB998900	ZWO	Old Dalby
024907	*	RDB998901	ZWO	Old Dalby
024908		DB998027	ZXP	Tyseley CS
024909	*	9106	BSOT	Preston Station
024910	*	210335	VDA	Toton TMD
024911		KDB770804	ZRV	Holyhead
024912		201058	VDA	Carlisle Upperby CWMD
024914		84114	NDV	Derby Etches Park T&RSMD
024915		ADB760617	ZDV	Speke Sidings, Garston
024916	*	ADB951496	ZSQ	BRML Wolverton
024917	*	ADB953408	ZSQ	BRML Wolverton
024918		93402	NKV	Willesden Brent Sidings
024919		93697	NKV	Wembley CARMD
024920	*	ADM700726	ZSV	Toton WRD
024921		93822	NKV	Longsight TMD
024922	*	ADB954014	ZSQ	Birkenhead North T&RSMD
024923		DB777171	ZDV	Northampton Castle Yard
024924	*	B310063	MDV	Tyseley TMD
024925		DB999093	ZRO	Tyseley TMD
024926		84390	NDV	Carlisle Upperby CWMD

024927		84332	NDV	Euston Down CS
024928	*	ADE230963	ZVW	Tyseley TMD
024929		110600	OBA	CMB Foodcans, Westhoughton
024930		110798	OBA	CMB Foodcans, Westhoughton
024931		B290050	MDO	British Steel, Shotton
024932		B290073	MDO	British Steel, Shotton
024933		B290183	MDO	British Steel, Shotton
024934		B290093	MDO	British Steel, Shotton
024935		B290190	MDO	British Steel, Shotton
024936		B290326	MDO	British Steel, Shotton
024949	*	59389	TSL	Tyseley TMD - grounded
024950		DB986948	ZBO	Chester WRD
024951		DB990559	ZBO	Chester WRD
024952		DB984552	ZBO	Chester WRD
024953		93682	NKV	Derby Etches Park T&RSMD
024955		201052	VDA	Derby Etches Park T&RSMD
024956		201064	VDA	Derby Etches Park T&RSMD
024957		ESS066317	TTA	Derby Etches Park T&RSMD
024958		ESS066135	TTA	Derby Etches Park T&RSMD
024959	*	KDB783354	ZRW	Crewe Gresty Road S&T Yard
024960	*	KDB783688	ZRW	Crewe Gresty Road S&T Yard
024961	*	KDB784199	ZRW	Crewe Gresty Road S&T Yard
024962	*	KDB784281	ZRW	Crewe Gresty Road S&T Yard
024963	*	KDB784455	ZRW	Crewe Gresty Road S&T Yard
024964	*	KDB783082	ZRW	Crewe Gresty Road S&T Yard
024965		RDB975036	QXV	RTC Derby
024966	*	KDB769490	ZDV	Crewe Gresty Road S&T Yard
024967		84146	NDV	Duddeston WRD
024968		DB990367	ZBO	Chester WRD
024969		KDB750268	ZRV	Derby S&T Sidings
024970	*	KDB977139	QRV	Crewe Gresty Road S&T Yard
024972	*	KDB977142	QRV	Crewe Gresty Road S&T Yard
024973	*	KDB769749	ZDV	Crewe Gresty Road S&T Yard
024974	*	KDB766019	ZDV	Crewe Gresty Road S&T Yard
024975		230140	VEA	Carlisle B Group CE Sidings
024976	*	210183	VDA	Toton Training School
024977	*	200843	VDA	Toton Training School
024978	*	200692	VDA	Toton Training School
024979	*	210139	VDA	Toton Training School
024980		KDB762855	ZRV	Leicester SD
024981		KDB773838	ZDV	Great Bridge Steel Terminal
024982		ADW44013	ZRV	Derby Etches Park T&RSMD
024983	*	ADB999054	ZRF	Tyseley TMD
024984	*	ADRS95000	ZOP	Toton TMD
024985	*	ADB933342	ZSV	Toton TMD
024986		ADC200376	ZRA	RTC Derby
024987		ADC200389	ZRA	RTC Derby
024988		ADC200406	ZRA	RTC Derby
024989	*	KDC200665	ZRA	Crewe Gresty Road S&T Yard
024990	*	KDC200668	ZRA	Crewe Gresty Road S&T Yard
024991	*	KDC200679	ZRA	Crewe Gresty Road S&T Yard
024992	*	KDC200888	ZRA	Crewe Gresty Road S&T Yard
024993		KDB741405	ZRV	Soho OHLM Depot
024994	*	ADB999080	ZRF	Derby Etches Park T&RSMD
024995	*	5421	TSO	MoD CAD Kineton
024996	*	5273	TSO	MoD CAD Kineton
024997	*	ADM395966	QXV	Crewe TMD (E)
024998		DB986610	ZBO	Dee Marsh
024999	*	ADB927826	YNV	Bescot TMD
025000	*	9423	BSO	Preston Station

025   (200216) TO   765968 TO   783838 TO   025036 TO
025   (210320) TO   780622 TO   025641 TO   025040 TO
                            783230 TO   025045 TO

025001 *	DB977181	QRV	Sandiacre Ballast Sidings
025002 *	DB977178	QRV	Sandiacre Ballast Sidings
025003 *	DB977179	QRV	Sandiacre Ballast Sidings
025004 *	DB977180	QRV	Sandiacre Ballast Sidings
025005 *	ADC200145	ZRB	Toton TMD

025016 ETCHES PK.   025017 CD   025018 CD   025030 STAFFORD
025006 DEE MARSH.   025025 EDGE HILL   025027 R.T.C. DERBY

Vehicles No Longer In Stock 025026 EDGE HILL
                                                  025031 TO
No.   Former Identity   Carkind 025028 TO   025032 TO
                                                  025033 SY

024400   B785023   VVV
Allocated to Speke Sidings, Garston. Scrapped at Speke Sidings, Garston by Phillips, Llanelli 9/88.

024401   B785742   VVV
Allocated to Speke Sidings, Garston. Scrapped at Speke Sidings, Garston by Phillips, Llanelli 9/88.

024402   B507283   FAV
Allocated to Crewe TMD. Scrapped at Crewe TMD by Poole, Stoke 5/84.

024403   B737688   FAV
Allocated to Hookagate Rail Welding Depot. Scrapped at Shrewsbury (Coton Hill) by Rollason, Telford 5/90.

024404   DW40071   YLO
Allocated to Fazakerley PAD. Scrapped at Fazakerley PAD by Bank Street Metals, Glossop 6/84.

024407   DM150756   ZQO
Allocated to Uttoxeter. Scrapped at Uttoxeter by Parkes, Oswestry 5/91.

024408   M31185   NFV
Allocated to Derby Litchurch Lane Works. Scrapped at Derby Litchurch Lane Works during 1987.

024409   M31344   NFV
Allocated to Derby Litchurch Lane Works. Scrapped at Derby Litchurch Lane Works during 1987.

024410   B767739   VVV
Allocated to Leicester Humberstone Road Yard. Scrapped at Leicester Humberstone Road Yard by Berry, Leicester 10/89.

024411   B931236   SPO
Allocated to Wembley CARMD. Scrapped at Coopers Metals, Sheffield 7/85.

024412   B930732   SPO
Allocated to Wembley CARMD. Scrapped at Coopers Metals, Sheffield 7/85.

024413   B930266   SPO
Allocated to Wembley CARMD. Scrapped at Coopers Metals, Sheffield 7/85.

024415   E306410   BDO
Allocated to Toton Yard. Scrapped at Wellingborough by Berry, Leicester 2/89.

024418   B773791   VVV
Allocated to Cricklewood TMD. Scrapped at Cricklewood TMD by Morris, Romford 2/89.

024419   B243755   MCO
Allocated to Cricklewood TMD. Broken up by BR at Cricklewood during 1986.

024420   B900813   XWP
Allocated to Hookagate Rail Welding Depot. Scrapped at Sheppards Waste Recovery, St. Helens 4/81.

024421   CDB506252   ZVV
Allocated to Wolverton Works. Scrapped at Wolverton Works during 1990.

024422   B387076   MSO
Allocated to Horwich Works. Scrapped at Horwich Works during 1983/84.

024425   TDB786577   ZDV
Allocated to Hawkesbury Lane. Scrapped at Ward Ferrous Metals, Stanton Gate 5/86.

024426   DB136442   ZHO
Allocated to Ditton Creosoting Depot. Believed scrapped at Ditton Creosoting Depot during 1985/6.

024427   B780905   VVV
Allocated to Three Spires Junction. Broken up by BR at Three Spires Junction 9/85.

024428   ADW2836   ZRV
Allocated to Carnforth On-Track Plant Depot. Scrapped at Sheppards, Seaforth 4/87.

024431   DW107177   YSV
Allocated to Derby Locomotive Works. Scrapped at Derby Locomotive Works 3/90.

024432   M31180   NFV
Allocated to Carlisle Currock WRD. Grounded. Scrapped at Carlisle Currock WRD during the first part of 1992.

024433   M31164   NFV
Allocated to Derby St. Andrews. Scrapped at Marple and Gillott, Sheffield 2/85.

<u>024435   B781300   VVV</u>
Allocated to Newton Heath TMD. Grounded at Newton Heath TMD 3/86. Sold to the East Lancashire Railway Preservation Society, Bury 1/87.

<u>024436   B780668   VVV</u>
Allocated to Newton Heath TMD. Grounded at Newton Heath TMD 3/86. Sold to the East Lancashire Railway Preservation Society, Bury 1/87.

024438   W94572   NPV
Allocated to Speke Sidings, Garston. Scrapped at Speke Sidings, Garston by Maize Metals, Wedmesbury 7/90.

024440   B781092   VVV
Allocated to Newton Heath TMD. Scrapped at Newton Heath TMD by Coopers Metals, Swindon 7/90.

024441   B777185   VVV
Allocated to Newton Heath TMD. Scrapped at Newton Heath TMD by Higgs, Barnsley 2/90.

024442   B778666   VVV
Allocated to Newton Heath TMD. Scrapped at Newton Heath TMD by Coopers Metals, Swindon 7/90.

024443   DB218160   ZHO
Allocated to Ditton Creosoting Depot.   Believed scrapped at Ditton Creosoting Depot by Lyon Bros, Liverpool 3/90.

024444   DB587169   ZHO
Allocated to Ditton Creosoting Depot.   Believed scrapped at Ditton Creosoting Depot during 1985/6.

024445   M31231   NFV
Allocated to Derby Litchurch Lane Works. Scrapped at Derby Litchurch Works during 1987.

024448   B882211   VVV
Allocated to Speke Sidings, Garston. Scrapped at Speke Sidings, Garston by Phillips, Llanelli 9/88.

024449   B786535   VVV
Allocated to Speke Sidings, Garston. Scrapped at Speke Sidings, Garston by Phillips, Llanelli 9/88.

024450   S220   NFV
Allocated to Tyseley TMD. Sold to Lewis, Coleshill (and currently stored at the Birmingham Railway Museum, Tyseley) 5/92.

024451   DB915017   ZSP
Allocated to Derby Locomotive Works. Scrapped at Derby Locomotive Works 3/90.

024452   DM322955   ZSP
Allocated to Derby Locomotive Works. Scrapped at Derby Locomotive Works 3/90.

024454   CDB460679   ZDO
Allocated to Crewe Works. Scrapped at Crewe Works during 1988/89.

024455   CDB33304   ZDO
Allocated to Crewe Works. Scrapped at Crewe Works during 1988/89.

024457   E94344   NPV
Allocated to Crewe On-Track Plant Depot.   Grounded 10/82. Sold to Jones, Talerdigg during the first part of 1987.

024460   M1780   RBR
Initially allocated to Heysham Harbour. Later Carlisle Upperby. Scrapped at Vic Berry, Leicester 3/88.

024462   M3954   TSO
Initially allocated to Heysham Harbour. Later Carlisle Upperby. Scrapped at Carlisle Upperby by Ward Ferrous Metals, Chepstow 11/87.

024465   S1478   NQV
Allocated to Railway Technical Centre, Derby. Scrapped at Railway Technical Centre, Derby by Rollason, Telford 11/86.

024466   B419719   HTO
Allocated to Derby Litchurch Lane Works. Scrapped at Derby Litchurch Lane Works 6/87.

024467   B412590   HTO
Allocated to Derby Litchurch Lane Works. Scrapped at Derby Litchurch Lane Works 6/87.

024468   B421841   HTO
Allocated to Derby Litchurch Lane Works. Scrapped at Derby Litchurch Lane Works
6/87.

024469   E270746   HTO
Allocated to Derby Litchurch Lane Works. Scrapped at Derby Litchurch Lane Works
6/87.

024470   B413033   HTO
Allocated to Derby Litchurch Lane Works. Scrapped at Derby Litchurch Lane Works
6/87.

024471   B411508   HTO
Allocated to Derby Litchurch Lane Works. Scrapped at Derby Litchurch Lane Works
6/87.

024472   B411384   HTO
Allocated to Derby Litchurch Lane Works. Scrapped at Derby Litchurch Lane Works
6/87.

024473   B410996   HTO
Allocated to Derby Litchurch Lane Works. Scrapped at Derby Litchurch Lane Works
6/87.

024474   E307300   HTO
Allocated to Derby Litchurch Lane Works. Scrapped at Derby Litchurch Lane Works
6/87.

024475   E307236   HTO
Allocated to Derby Litchurch Lane Works. Scrapped at Derby Litchurch Lane Works
6/87.

024476   M1639   RBR
Number initially allocated to HTO B411580 for use at Derby Litchurch Lane Works, but
subsequently cancelled the vehicle instead being sent to Coopers Metals, Handsworth.
Number reissued to M1639 for use at Euston Down CS. Later stored at Wembley CARMD.
Scrapped at Mayer Parry, Snailwell 11/91.

024477   B411144   HTO
Allocated to Derby Litchurch Lane Works. Scrapped at Derby Litchurch Lane Works
6/87.

024479   ADE310782   ZTO
Allocated to Penyffordd. Scrapped at Penyffordd by North Wales Metal, Wrexham 2/85.

024480   ADM395969   QVV
Allocated to Derby Litchurch Lane Works. Scrapped at Derby Litchurch Lane Works
during 1986.

024483   ADB757665   ZDV
Allocated to Shrewsbury Station. Scrapped at Shrewsbury (Coton Hill) by Rollason,
Telford 5/90.

024485   ADM395971   QVV
Allocated to Derby Litchurch Lane Works. Scrapped at Derby Litchurch Lane Works
during 1990.

024486   ADM395973   QVV
Allocated to Derby Litchurch Lane Works. Scrapped at Derby Litchurch Lane Works
during 1990.

024487   B476664   OHV
Allocated to Wolverton Works. Scrapped at Wolverton Works during the latter part of 1987.

024488   B478779   OHV
Allocated to Wolverton Works. Scrapped at Wolverton Works 2/89.

024489   B487792   OHV
Allocated to Wolverton Works. Scrapped at Wolverton Works 6/89.

024490   B492191   OHV
Allocated to Wolverton Works. Scrapped at Wolverton Works 6/89.

024491   B488977   OHV
Allocated to Wolverton Works. Scrapped at Wolverton Works 2/89.

024492   B489074   OHV
Allocated to Wolverton Works. Scrapped at Wolverton Works 6/89.

024493   B745522   OHV
Allocated to Wolverton Works. Sold to the East Anglian Railway Museum 1/88.

024494   B489208   OHV
Allocated to Wolverton Works. Scrapped at Wolverton Works 2/89.

024495   B489682   OHV
Allocated to Wolverton Works. Scrapped at Wolverton Works during the latter part of 1987.

024496   B487658   OHV
Allocated to Wolverton Works. Scrapped at Wolverton Works 6/89.

024498   M1749   RBR
Allocated to Edge Hill CARMD. Scrapped at Berry, Leicester 9/89.

024502   CDB704979   ZVV
Allocated to Derby Locomotive Works. Scrapped at Derby Locomotive Works by Ward Ferrous Metals, Ilkeston 4/86.

024503   CDB704918   ZVV
Allocated to Derby Locomotive Works. Scrapped at Derby Locomotive Works 3/90.

024504   CDB709822   ZVV
Allocated to Derby Locomotive Works. Scrapped at Derby Locomotive Works 3/90.

024506   B931545   SPV
Allocated to Chester WRD. Broken up by BR at Chester WRD 10/91.

024513   DM231272   ZQV
Allocated to Stoke Cockshute. Scrapped at Stoke Cockshute by Ward Ferrous Metals, Sheffield 7/84.

024517   B730508   STV
Allocated to Ditton Creosoting Depot. Scrapped at Ditton Creosoting Depot by Howard and Wheeler, Ecclesfield 10/87.

024518   B730549   STV
Allocated to Ditton Creosoting Depot. Scrapped at Ditton Creosoting Depot by Howard and Wheeler, Ecclesfield 10/87.

024519   B732113   STV
Allocated to Ditton Creosoting Depot.   Scrapped at Ditton Creosoting Depot by Howard
and Wheeler, Ecclesfield 10/87.

024520   B732836   STV
Allocated to Ditton Creosoting Depot.   Scrapped at Ditton Creosoting Depot by Howard
and Wheeler, Ecclesfield 10/87.

024521   B732882   STV
Allocated to Ditton Creosoting Depot.   Scrapped at Ditton Creosoting Depot by Howard
and Wheeler, Ecclesfield 10/87.

024522   DB730821   ZDV
Allocated to Ditton Creosoting Depot.   Scrapped at Ditton Creosoting Depot by Howard
and Wheeler, Ecclesfield 10/87.

024523   DB732022   ZDV
Allocated to Ditton Creosoting Depot.   Scrapped at Ditton Creosoting Depot by Howard
and Wheeler, Ecclesfield 10/87.

024524   DB732326   ZDV
Allocated to Ditton Creosoting Depot.   Scrapped at Ditton Creosoting Depot by Taylor
Bros., Bury 6/87.

024525   DB732350   ZDV
Allocated to Ditton Creosoting Depot.   Scrapped at Ditton Creosoting Depot by Howard
and Wheeler, Ecclesfield 10/87.

024526   DB732782   ZDV
Allocated to Ditton Creosoting Depot.   Scrapped at Ditton Creosoting Depot by Howard
and Wheeler, Ecclesfield 10/87.

024527   DB732943   ZDV
Allocated to Ditton Creosoting Depot.   Scrapped at Ditton Creosoting Depot by Howard
and Wheeler, Ecclesfield 10/87.

024528   B732592   STV
Allocated to Ditton Creosoting Depot.. Scrapped at Ditton Creosoting Depot by Howard
and Wheeler, Ecclesfield 10/87.

024532   ADM201017   ZVV
Allocated to Toton TMD. Sold from Toton TMD to the Midland Railway Trust, Butterley
8/91.

024538   DB932546   ZDV
Allocated to Walsall Tasker Street.   Scrapped at Sheppards, Seaforth 7/87.

024539   DB935281   ZDV
Allocated to Walsall Tasker Street.   Scrapped at Sheppards, Seaforth 7/87.

024540   DB935368   ZDV
Allocated to Walsall Tasker Street.   Scrapped at Coopers Metals, Handsworth 12/88.

024541   DB935373   ZDV
Allocated to Walsall Tasker Street.   Scrapped at Coopers Metals, Handsworth 12/88.

024542   DB935437   ZDV
Allocated to Walsall Tasker Street.   Scrapped at Sheppards, Seaforth 7/87.

024544   DB935907   ZDV
Allocated to Walsall Tasker Street.   Scrapped at Sheppards, Seaforth 7/87.

024545   DB936003   ZDV
Allocated to Walsall Tasker Street.   Scrapped at Sheppards, Seaforth 7/87.

024547   DB936139   ZDV
Allocated to Walsall Tasker Street.   Scrapped at Sheppards, Seaforth 7/87.

024549   DB936191   ZDV
Allocated to Walsall Tasker Street.   Scrapped at Coopers Metals, Handsworth 12/88.

024550   DB936240   ZDV
Allocated to Walsall Tasker Street.   Scrapped at Coopers Metals, Handsworth 12/88.

024551   DB936244   ZDV
Allocated to Walsall Tasker Street.   Scrapped at Coopers Metals, Handsworth 12/88.

024552   DB936264   ZDV
Allocated to Walsall Tasker Street.   Scrapped at Coopers Metals, Handsworth 12/88.

024554   DB936381   ZDV
Allocated to Walsall Tasker Street.   Scrapped at Coopers Metals, Handsworth 12/88.

024555   DB936386   ZDV
Allocated to Walsall Tasker Street.   Scrapped at Sheppards, Seaforth 7/87.

024556   DB936441   ZDV
Allocated to Walsall Tasker Street.   Scrapped at Sheppards, Seaforth 7/87.

024557   DB934063   ZDV
Allocated to Castleton CMD. Scrapped at Sheppards Waste Recovery, St. Helens Junction 4/86.

024558   DB935236   ZDV
Allocated to Castleton CMD. Scrapped at Sheppards Waste Recovery, St. Helens Junction 4/86.

024559   DB935361   ZDV
Allocated to Castleton CMD. Scrapped at Sheppards Waste Recovery, St. Helens Junction 4/86.

024560   DB935397   ZDV
Allocated to Castleton CMD. Scrapped at Sheppards Waste Recovery, St. Helens Junction 4/86.

024561   DB935502   ZDV
Allocated to Castleton CMD. Scrapped at Coopers Metals, Sheffield 2/89.

024563   DB935557   ZDV
Allocated to Castleton CMD. Scrapped at Sheppards Waste Recovery, St. Helens Junction 4/86.

024564   DB935673   ZDV
Allocated to Castleton CMD. Scrapped at Sheppards Waste Recovery, St. Helens Junction 4/86.

024565   DB935681   ZDV
Allocated to Castleton CMD. Scrapped at Sheppards Waste Recovery, St. Helens Junction 4/86.

024566   DB935751   ZDV
Allocated to Castleton CMD. Scrapped at Sheppards Waste Recovery, St. Helens Junction 4/86.

024567   DB935760   ZDV
Allocated to Castleton CMD. Scrapped at Sheppards Waste Recovery, St. Helens Junction 4/86.

024568   DB935770   ZDV
Allocated to Castleton CMD. Scrapped at Sheppards Waste Recovery, St. Helens Junction 4/86.

024569   DB935846   ZDV
Allocated to Castleton CMD. Scrapped at Sheppards Waste Recovery, St. Helens Junction 4/86.

024572   DB935995   ZDV
Allocated to Castleton CMD. Scrapped at Sheppards Waste Recovery, St. Helens Junction 4/86.

024574   DB936060   ZDV
Allocated to Castleton CMD. Scrapped at Sheppards Waste Recovery, St. Helens Junction 4/86.

024575   DB936088   ZDV
Allocated to Castleton CMD. Scrapped at Sheppards Waste Recovery, St. Helens Junction 4/86.

024577   DB936125   ZDV
Allocated to Castleton CMD. Scrapped at Sheppards Waste Recovery, St. Helens Junction 4/86.

024578   DB936217   ZDV
Allocated to Castleton CMD. Scrapped at Coopers Metals, Sheffield 2/89.

024579   DB936434   ZDV
Allocated to Castleton CMD. Scrapped at Sheppards Waste Recovery, St. Helens Junction 4/86.

024580   DB936480   ZDV
Allocated to Castleton CMD. Scrapped at Sheppards Waste Recovery, St. Helens Junction 4/86.

024581   DB936506   ZDV
Allocated to Castleton CMD. Scrapped at Sheppards Waste Recovery, St. Helens Junction 4/86.

024582   DB935189   ZDV
Allocated to Fazakerley PAD. Sold to Sheppards Waste Recovery, Alexandra Dock, Liverpool and moved to Edge Hill 11/87. Stored at Edge Hill and then Spekeland Road Freight Depot pending settlement of a contractual dispute. Scrapped at Spekeland Road Freight Depot by Sheppard (Group), Southampton 9/91.

024583   DB935366   ZDV
Allocated to Fazakerley PAD. Sold to Sheppards Waste Recovery, Alexandra Dock, Liverpool and moved to Edge Hill 11/87. Stored at Edge Hill and then Spekeland Road Freight Depot pending settlement of a contractual dispute. Scrapped at Spekeland Road Freight Depot by Sheppard (Group), Southampton 9/91.

024584   DB935398   ZDV
Allocated to Fazakerley PAD. Sold to Sheppards Waste Recovery, Alexandra Dock,
Liverpool and moved to Edge Hill 11/87. Stored at Edge Hill and then Spekeland Road
Freight Depot pending settlement of a contractual dispute. Scrapped at Spekeland
Road Freight Depot by Sheppard (Group), Southampton 9/91.

024585   DB935474   ZDV
Allocated to Fazakerley PAD. Sold to Sheppards Waste Recovery, Alexandra Dock,
Liverpool and moved to Edge Hill 11/87. Stored at Edge Hill and then Spekeland Road
Freight Depot pending settlement of a contractual dispute. Scrapped at Spekeland
Road Freight Depot by Sheppard (Group), Southampton 9/91.

024586   DB935561   ZDV
Allocated to Fazakerley PAD. Sold to Sheppards Waste Recovery, Alexandra Dock,
Liverpool and moved to Edge Hill 11/87. Stored at Edge Hill and then Spekeland Road
Freight Depot pending settlement of a contractual dispute. Scrapped at Spekeland
Road Freight Depot by Sheppard (Group), Southampton 9/91.

024587   DB935579   ZDV
Allocated to Fazakerley PAD. Sold to Sheppards Waste Recovery, Alexandra Dock,
Liverpool and moved to Edge Hill 11/87. Stored at Edge Hill and then Spekeland Road
Freight Depot pending settlement of a contractual dispute. Scrapped at Spekeland
Road Freight Depot by Sheppard (Group), Southampton 9/91.

024588   DB935674   ZDV
Allocated to Fazakerley PAD. Sold to Sheppards Waste Recovery, Alexandra Dock,
Liverpool and moved to Edge Hill 11/87. Stored at Edge Hill and then Spekeland Road
Freight Depot pending settlement of a contractual dispute. Scrapped at Spekeland
Road Freight Depot by Sheppard (Group), Southampton 9/91.

024589   DB935761   ZDV
Allocated to Fazakerley PAD. Sold to Sheppards Waste Recovery, Alexandra Dock,
Liverpool and moved to Edge Hill 11/87. Stored at Edge Hill and then Spekeland Road
Freight Depot pending settlement of a contractual dispute. Scrapped at Spekeland
Road Freight Depot by Sheppard (Group), Southampton 9/91.

024590   DB935834   ZDV
Allocated to Fazakerley PAD. Sold to Sheppards Waste Recovery, Alexandra Dock,
Liverpool and moved to Edge Hill 11/87. Stored at Edge Hill and then Spekeland Road
Freight Depot pending settlement of a contractual dispute. Scrapped at Spekeland
Road Freight Depot by Sheppard (Group), Southampton 9/91.

024591   DB935867   ZDV
Allocated to Fazakerley PAD. Sold to Sheppards Waste Recovery, Alexandra Dock,
Liverpool and moved to Edge Hill 11/87. Stored at Edge Hill and then Spekeland Road
Freight Depot pending settlement of a contractual dispute. Scrapped at Spekeland
Road Freight Depot by Sheppard (Group), Southampton 9/91.

024592   DB935909   ZDV
Allocated to Fazakerley PAD. Sold to Sheppards Waste Recovery, Alexandra Dock,
Liverpool and moved to Edge Hill 11/87. Stored at Edge Hill and then Spekeland Road
Freight Depot pending settlement of a contractual dispute. Scrapped at Spekeland
Road Freight Depot by Sheppard (Group), Southampton 9/91.

024593   DB935934   ZDV
Allocated to Fazakerley PAD. Sold to Sheppards Waste Recovery, Alexandra Dock,
Liverpool and moved to Edge Hill 11/87. Stored at Edge Hill and then Spekeland Road
Freight Depot pending settlement of a contractual dispute. Scrapped at Spekeland
Road Freight Depot by Sheppard (Group), Southampton 9/91.

024594   DB935968   ZDV
Allocated to Fazakerley PAD. Sold to Sheppards Waste Recovery, Alexandra Dock, Liverpool and moved to Edge Hill 11/87. Stored at Edge Hill and then Spekeland Road Freight Depot pending settlement of a contractual dispute. Scrapped at Spekeland Road Freight Depot by Sheppard (Group), Southampton 9/91.

024595   DB936100   ZDV
Allocated to Fazakerley PAD. Sold to Sheppards Waste Recovery, Alexandra Dock, Liverpool and moved to Edge Hill 11/87. Stored at Edge Hill and then Spekeland Road Freight Depot pending settlement of a contractual dispute. Scrapped at Spekeland Road Freight Depot by Sheppard (Group), Southampton 9/91.

024596   DB936126   ZDV
Allocated to Fazakerley PAD. Sold to Sheppards Waste Recovery, Alexandra Dock, Liverpool and moved to Edge Hill 11/87. Stored at Edge Hill and then Spekeland Road Freight Depot pending settlement of a contractual dispute. Scrapped at Spekeland Road Freight Depot by Sheppard (Group), Southampton 9/91.

024597   DB936385   ZDV
Allocated to Fazakerley PAD. Sold to Sheppards Waste Recovery, Alexandra Dock, Liverpool and moved to Edge Hill 11/87. Stored at Edge Hill and then Spekeland Road Freight Depot pending settlement of a contractual dispute. Scrapped at Spekeland Road Freight Depot by Sheppard (Group), Southampton 9/91.

024598   DB936391   ZDV
Allocated to Fazakerley PAD. Sold to Sheppards Waste Recovery, Alexandra Dock, Liverpool and moved to Edge Hill 11/87. Stored at Edge Hill and then Spekeland Road Freight Depot pending settlement of a contractual dispute. Scrapped at Spekeland Road Freight Depot by Sheppard (Group), Southampton 9/91.

024599   DB936420   ZDV
Allocated to Fazakerley PAD. Sold to Sheppards Waste Recovery, Alexandra Dock, Liverpool and moved to Edge Hill 11/87. Stored at Edge Hill and then Spekeland Road Freight Depot pending settlement of a contractual dispute. Scrapped at Spekeland Road Freight Depot by Sheppard (Group), Southampton 9/91.

024600   DB936459   ZDV
Allocated to Fazakerley PAD. Sold to Sheppards Waste Recovery, Alexandra Dock, Liverpool and moved to Edge Hill 11/87. Stored at Edge Hill and then Spekeland Road Freight Depot pending settlement of a contractual dispute. Scrapped at Spekeland Road Freight Depot by Sheppard (Group), Southampton 9/91.

024601   DB936515   ZDV
Allocated to Fazakerley PAD. Sold to Sheppards Waste Recovery, Alexandra Dock, Liverpool and moved to Edge Hill 11/87. Stored at Edge Hill and then Spekeland Road Freight Depot pending settlement of a contractual dispute. Scrapped at Spekeland Road Freight Depot by Sheppard (Group), Southampton 9/91.

024602   -   -
Number issued to SUKO83122 but subsequently cancelled. See 024500.

024604   ADM40292   QRV
Allocated to Crewe TMD. Scrapped at Crewe TMD by Casbern Metals, Stoke 10/86.

024605   ADM40300   QRV
Allocated to Crewe TMD. Scrapped at Crewe TMD by Casbern Metals, Stoke 10/86.

024608   M94395   NPV
Initially allocated to Holyhead. Later Preston Dock Street. Scrapped at Preston Dock Street by Rollason, Telford 3/89.

024609   M94149   NPV
Allocated to Derby Etches Park T&RSMD. Later stored at Nottingham CS. Scrapped at Mayer Parry, Snailwell 5/91.

024610   M94605   NPV
Allocated to Derby Etches Park T&RSMD. Later stored at Nottingham CS. Sold from Nottingham CS to the Deltic Preservation Society at the Great Central Railway 12/90.

024612   B462738   RFQ
Allocated to Wolverton Works. Scrapped at Wolverton Works 2/89.

024613   B462718   RFQ
Allocated to Wolverton Works. Scrapped at Wolverton Works during 1990.

024614   B932246   SPV
Allocated to Derby Etches Park T&RSMD. Scrapped at Wellingborough by Berry, Leicester 2/89.

024616   B935758   SPV
Allocated to Derby Etches Park T&RSMD. Scrapped at Derby Locomotive Works 3/90.

024618   B315261   MDO
Allocated to Crewe Works. Scrapped at Crewe Works during 1988/89.

024619   B315853   MDO
Allocated to Crewe Works. Scrapped at Crewe Works during 1988/89.

024621   B315933   MDO
Allocated to Crewe Works. Scrapped at Crewe Works during 1988/89.

024622   B317243   MDO
Allocated to Crewe Works. Scrapped at Crewe Works during 1988/89.

024624   M94891   NPV
Allocated to Fazakerley PAD. Scrapped at Fazakerley PAD by Rollason, Telford 7/87.

024625   DB994540   YBO
Allocated to Fazakerley PAD. Scrapped at Fazakerley PAD by Trackwork, Doncaster 2/88.

024626   DB994563   YBO
Allocated to Fazakerley PAD. Scrapped at Fazakerley PAD by Trackwork, Doncaster 2/88.

024627   DB994600   YBO
Allocated to Fazakerley PAD. Scrapped at Fazakerley PAD by Trackwork, Doncaster 2/88.

024628   DB994611   YBO
Allocated to Fazakerley PAD. Scrapped at Fazakerley PAD by Trackwork, Doncaster 2/88.

024629   DB994541   YBO
Allocated to Fazakerley PAD. Scrapped at Fazakerley PAD by Trackwork, Doncaster 2/88.

024630   DB994569   YBO
Allocated to Fazakerley PAD. Scrapped at Fazakerley PAD by Trackwork, Doncaster 2/88.

```
024631          DB994607        YBO
Allocated to    Fazakerley PAD.  Scrapped at Fazakerley PAD by Trackwork, Doncaster
2/88.

024632          DB994558        YBO
Allocated to    Fazakerley PAD.  Scrapped at Fazakerley PAD by Trackwork, Doncaster
2/88.

024633          DB994588        YBO
Allocated to    Fazakerley PAD.  Scrapped at Fazakerley PAD by Trackwork, Doncaster
2/88.

024634          DB994608        YBO
Allocated to    Fazakerley PAD.  Scrapped at Fazakerley PAD by Trackwork, Doncaster
2/88.

024636          DM721049        YBO
Allocated to    Fazakerley PAD.  Scrapped at Fazakerley PAD by Trackwork, Doncaster
2/88.

024637          B931513         SEV
Allocated to Wolverton Works.  Scrapped at Wolverton Works during the latter part of
1987.

024638          B933089         SEV
Allocated to Wolverton Works.  Scrapped at Wolverton Works 2/89.

024639          B933169         SEV
Allocated to Wolverton Works. Scrapped at Wolverton Works 2/89.

024640          B933261         SEV
Allocated to Wolverton Works. Scrapped at Wolverton Works 2/89.

024641          B933403         SEV
Allocated to Wolverton Works. Scrapped at Wolverton Works during 1990.

024642          B933427         SEV
Allocated to Wolverton Works. Scrapped at Wolverton Works 6/89.

024643          B933584         SEV
Allocated to Wolverton Works. Scrapped at Wolverton Works during 1990.

024644          B933699         SEV
Allocated to Wolverton Works. Scrapped at Wolverton Works 6/89.

024645          B933726         SEV
Allocated to Wolverton Works. Scrapped at Wolverton Works 2/89.

024646          B934378         SEV
Allocated to Wolverton Works. Scrapped at Wolverton Works 2/89.

024647          B934545         SEV
Allocated to Wolverton Works. Scrapped at Wolverton Works during 1990.

024648          B935611         SEV
Allocated to Wolverton Works. Scrapped at Wolverton Works 2/89.

024649          B935802         SEV
Allocated to Wolverton Works. Scrapped at Wolverton Works 6/89.
```

024650   B936356   SEV
Allocated to Wolverton Works. Scrapped at Wolverton Works 6/89.

024651   B936484   SEV
Allocated to Wolverton Works. Scrapped at Wolverton Works 2/89.

024652   DB994542   YBO
Allocated to Fazakerley PAD.   Scrapped at Fazakerley PAD by Trackwork, Doncaster 2/88.

024653   DB994556   YBO
Allocated to Fazakerley PAD.   Scrapped at Fazakerley PAD by Trackwork, Doncaster 2/88.

024654   DB994571   YBO
Allocated to Fazakerley PAD.   Scrapped at Fazakerley PAD by Trackwork, Doncaster 2/88.

024657   B462724   RFQ
Allocated to Wolverton Works. Scrapped at Wolverton Works 2/89.

024658   B462720   RFQ
Allocated to Wolverton Works. Scrapped at Wolverton Works 2/89.

024659   B462736   RFQ
Allocated to Wolverton Works. Scrapped at Wolverton Works during 1990.

024660   B462767   RFQ
Allocated to Wolverton Works.   Scrapped at Wolverton Works during the latter part of 1987.

024661   B462774   RFQ
Allocated to Wolverton Works. Scrapped at Wolverton Works 2/89.

024662   B462789   RFQ
Allocated to Wolverton Works. Scrapped at Wolverton Works during 1990.

024663   B462751   RFQ
Allocated to Derby Litchurch Lane   Works.   Scrapped at Derby Litchurch Lane Works during 1991.

024665   M94410   NPV
Allocated to Toton TMD. Scrapped at Booth Roe Metals, Rotherham 8/91.

024667   ADB975197   QRV
Allocated to Derby Etches Park T&RSMD.   Later stored at Nottingham CS. Scrapped at Mayer Parry, Snailwell 5/91.

024668   ADB975198   QRV
Allocated to Derby Etches Park T&RSMD.   Later stored at Nottingham CS. Scrapped at Mayer Parry, Snailwell 5/91.

024673   DE312209   ZGV
Allocated to Northampton Castle Yard. Scrapped at Coopers Metals, Handsworth 7/90.

024675   CDB932916   ZRV
Allocated to Derby Litchurch Lane   Works.   Scrapped at Derby Litchurch Lane Works during 1990.

The privatisation of BREL has resulted in a drastic reduction in the fleet of internal users at BREL sites. One vintage survivor is 024330 (formerly GWR tank W43930) pictured at BREL Crewe on 21st July 1990. Paul W. Bartlett

Once a common sight in BR freight trains, the standard 12 ton van now only survives in the internal user fleet. 024424, pictured at Derby Etches Park T&RSMD on 2nd May 1992, is a typical example. C. J. Tuffs

It is very rare for either a DMU or EMU to be taken into the internal user fleet. One exception is 024949 (number not yet carried) seen here at Tyseley TMD on 7th September 1991.   Steve Knight

The internal user fleet contains a variety of tank wagons including 041406 seen in this photograph at Immingham TMD on 7th September 1986.   Bob Wallace

024676   CDB708489   ZVV
Allocated to Wolverton Works. Scrapped at Wolverton Works 10/89.

024677   CDB932624   ZRV
Allocated to Wolverton Works. Scrapped at Wolverton Works 6/89.

024678   CDB934498   ZRV
Allocated to Wolverton Works. Scrapped at Wolverton Works 2/89.

024679   CDB935020   ZRV
Allocated to Wolverton Works. Scrapped at Wolverton Works 2/89.

024680   CDB934644   ZRV
Allocated to Wolverton Works. Scrapped at Wolverton Works during 1990.

024685   -   -
Number issued to B462712 for use at Derby Litchurch Lane Works but subsequently cancelled, the vehicle remaining in Capital Stock use at Trafford Park FLT.

024686   -   -
Number issued to B462735 for use at Derby Litchurch Lane Works but subsequently cancelled, the vehicle remaining in Capital Stock use at Willesden FLT. Vehicle now stored awaiting disposal at Wembley CARMD.

024687   B745187   FVW
Allocated to Birmingham Lawley Street FLT. Later Wolverhampton Steel Terminal. Scrapped at Wolverhampton Steel Terminal by Coopers Metals, Bilston 4/91.

024689   B745010   FVV
Allocated to Derby Litchurch Lane Works. Scrapped at Derby Litchurch Lane Works during 1990.

024691   B745038   FVV
Allocated to Derby Litchurch Lane Works. Scrapped at Derby Litchurch Lane Works during 1990.

024692   B745054   FVV
Allocated to Derby Litchurch Lane Works. Scrapped at Derby Litchurch Lane Works during 1990.

024693   B745068   FVV
Allocated to Derby Litchurch Lane Works. Scrapped at Derby Litchurch Lane Works during 1990.

024694   B745608   FVV
Allocated to Derby Litchurch Lane Works. Scrapped at Derby Litchurch Lane Works during 1990.

024698   DB996034   YMO
Allocated to Derby Litchurch Lane Works. Scrapped at Derby Litchurch Lane Works during 1990.

024699   DB996046   YMO
Allocated to Derby Litchurch Lane Works. Scrapped at Derby Litchurch Lane Works during 1990.

024700   DB996053   YMO
Allocated to Derby Litchurch Lane Works. Scrapped at Derby Litchurch Lane Works during 1990.

024702   DB996156   YMO
Allocated to Derby Litchurch Lane Works. Scrapped at Derby Litchurch Lane Works during 1990.

024704   DB996060   YMO
Allocated to Fazakerley PAD. Scrapped at Fazakerley PAD by Trackwork, Doncaster 2/88.

024705   DB996055   YMO
Allocated to Fazakerley PAD. Scrapped at Fazakerley PAD by Trackwork, Doncaster 2/88.

024706   DB996158   YMO
Allocated to Fazakerley PAD. Scrapped at Fazakerley PAD by Trackwork, Doncaster 2/88.

024707   DB996038   YMO
Allocated to Fazakerley PAD. Scrapped at Fazakerley PAD by Trackwork, Doncaster 2/88.

024708   DB996208   YMO
Allocated to Fazakerley PAD. Scrapped at Fazakerley PAD by Trackwork, Doncaster 2/88.

024718   DB996037   YMO
Allocated to Derby Litchurch Lane Works. Scrapped at Derby Litchurch Lane Works during 1990.

024719   M93923   NKV
Allocated to Chester WRD. Scrapped at Booth Roe Metals, Rotherham 5/89.

024740   DB589525   ZHV
Allocated to Ditton Creosoting Depot. Scrapped at Ditton Creosoting Depot by Lyon Bros (Metals), Liverpool 3/90.

024742   S1865   NQV
Allocated an internal user number in order to remove vehicle from revenue fleet. Sold from Toton WRD to the Midland Railway Trust, Butterley 6/87.

024745   ADB853341   ZDV
Allocated to RTC Derby. Scrapped at RTC Derby by Barrett, Sheffield 12/88.

024746   ADB853964   ZDV
Allocated to RTC Derby. Scrapped at RTC Derby by Barrett, Sheffield 12/88.

024748   ADB875654   ZXV
Allocated to RTC Derby. Scrapped at RTC Derby by Barrett, Sheffield 12/88.

024749   ADB875662   ZXV
Allocated to RTC Derby. Scrapped at RTC Derby by Barrett, Sheffield 12/88.

024750   ADB875763   ZXV
Allocated to RTC Derby. Scrapped at RTC Derby by Barrett, Sheffield 12/88.

024751   ADB875835   ZXV
Allocated to RTC Derby. Scrapped at RTC Derby by Barrett, Sheffield 12/88.

024758   TDB931856   ZSQ
Allocated to Doe Hill. Sold from Doe Hill to the Midland Railway Trust, Butterley during 1987/88.

024763   ADB786797   ZDV
Allocated to Toton TMD. Believed scrapped at Toton TMD during the latter part of 1987.

024764   -   -
Number issued to ADB761561 but subsequently cancelled. See 024798.

024766   -   -
Number issued to ADB999054 but subsequently cancelled. See 024983.

024768   -   -
Number issued to ADB999016 but subsequently cancelled. See 024765.

024769   DB730867   ZAV
Allocated to Ditton Creosoting Depot. Scrapped at Ditton Creosoting Depot by Lyon Bros (Metals), Liverpool 3/90.

024770   DB732752   ZAV
Allocated to Ditton Creosoting Depot. Scrapped at Ditton Creosoting Depot by Lyon Bros (Metals), Liverpool 3/90.

024771   DB731746   ZAV
Allocated to Ditton Creosoting Depot. Scrapped at Ditton Creosoting Depot by Lyon Bros (Metals), Liverpool 3/90.

024772   DB732894   ZAV
Allocated to Ditton Creosoting Depot. Scrapped at Ditton Creosoting Depot by Lyon Bros (Metals), Liverpool 3/90.

024773   DB732950   ZAV
Allocated to Ditton Creosoting Depot. Scrapped at Ditton Creosoting Depot by Lyon Bros (Metals), Liverpool 3/90.

024774   DB732379   ZAV
Allocated to Ditton Creosoting Depot. Scrapped at Ditton Creosoting Depot by Lyon Bros (Metals), Liverpool 3/90.

024775   DB730237   ZAV
Allocated to Ditton Creosoting Depot. Scrapped at Ditton Creosoting Depot by Lyon Bros (Metals), Liverpool 3/90.

024776   DB732226   ZAV
Allocated to Ditton Creosoting Depot. Scrapped at Ditton Creosoting Depot by Lyon Bros (Metals), Liverpool 3/90.

024777   DB733187   ZAV
Allocated to Ditton Creosoting Depot. Scrapped at Ditton Creosoting Depot by Lyon Bros (Metals), Liverpool 3/90.

024778   DB733380   ZAV
Allocated to Ditton Creosoting Depot. Scrapped at Ditton Creosoting Depot by Lyon Bros (Metals), Liverpool 3/90.

024779   DB732182   ZAV
Allocated to Ditton Creosoting Depot. Scrapped at Ditton Creosoting Depot by Lyon Bros (Metals), Liverpool 3/90.

024781   KDB948044   YRV
Allocated to Wolverton Station. Reinstated to the departmental fleet as KDB948044 9/90. Now stored at BRML Wolverton.

024782   KDB948073   YRV
Allocated to Wolverton Station. Reinstated to the departmental fleet as KDB948073 9/90. Now stored at BRML Wolverton.

024785   -   -
Number issued to 93913 but subsequently cancelled. See 024890.

024786   -   -
Number issued to 93682 but subsequently cancelled. See 024953.

024788   TDB932084   ZSR
Allocated to Carlisle Currock WRD. To Chester WRD for possible reinstatement to the departmental fleet as KDB932084. Broken up by BR at Chester WRD 9/89.

024789   -   -
Number issued to TDB932434 but subsequently cancelled. See 024871.

024790   -   -
Number issued to DB740323 for use at Holyhead but subsequently cancelled, the vehicle instead being scrapped at Sheppards, Seaforth 9/87.

024800   ADB721587   ZGV
Allocated to Duddeston WRD. Sold from Duddeston WRD to the Great Central Railway 6/92.

024803   -   -
Number issued to ADB999016 but subsequently cancelled. See 024765.

024819   DE250470   ZSP
Allocated to Chester WRD. Broken up by BR at Chester WRD 10/91.

024870   ADS39599   ZDV
Allocated for use at Tyseley TMD but never reached there. Stored at Woking and then Eastleigh Field Sidings. Scrapped at Coopers Metals, Handsworth 4/92.

024873   CDB506340   ZVV
Allocated to Wolverton Works. Scrapped at Wolverton Works during 1990.

024876   CDB506759   ZVV
Allocated to Wolverton Works. Scrapped at Wolverton Works during 1990.

024879   CDB502996   ZVV
Allocated to Wolverton Works. Scrapped at Wolverton Works during 1990.

024882   CDB507045   ZVV
Allocated to Wolverton Works. Scrapped at Wolverton Works during 1990.

024889   93392   NKV
Allocated to Derby Etches Park. Scrapped at Booth Roe Metals, Rotherham 2/91.

024892   DB733074   *   ZAV
Allocated to Ditton Creosoting Depot. Scrapped at Ditton Creosoting Depot by Queenborough Railway Materials, Renishaw 4/92.

024893   DB732013   ZAV
Allocated to Ditton Creosoting Depot. Scrapped at Ditton Creosoting Depot by Queenborough Railway Materials, Renishaw 4/92.

024894   DB733087   ZAV
Allocated to Ditton Creosoting Depot. Scrapped at Ditton Creosoting Depot by Queenborough Railway Materials, Renishaw 4/92.

024895   DB731853   ZAV
Allocated to Ditton Creosoting Depot. Scrapped at Ditton Creosoting Depot by Queenborough Railway Materials, Renishaw 4/92.

024896   DB732685   ZAV
Allocated to Ditton Creosoting Depot. Scrapped at Ditton Creosoting Depot by Queenborough Railway Materials, Renishaw 4/92.

024897   DB733314   ZAV
Allocated to Ditton Creosoting Depot. Scrapped at Ditton Creosoting Depot by Queenborough Railway Materials, Renishaw 4/92.

024898   DB732447   ZAV
Allocated to Ditton Creosoting Depot. Scrapped at Ditton Creosoting Depot by Queenborough Railway Materials, Renishaw 4/92.

024899   DB731980   ZAV
Allocated to Ditton Creosoting Depot. Scrapped at Ditton Creosoting Depot by Queenborough Railway Materials, Renishaw 4/92.

024900   DB730597   ZAV
Allocated to Ditton Creosoting Depot. Scrapped at Ditton Creosoting Depot by Queenborough Railway Materials, Renishaw 4/92.

024901   DB730852   ZAV
Allocated to Ditton Creosoting Depot. Scrapped at Ditton Creosoting Depot by Queenborough Railway Materials, Renishaw 4/92.

024902   DB731786   ZAV
Allocated to Ditton Creosoting Depot. Scrapped at Ditton Creosoting Depot by Queenborough Railway Materials, Renishaw 4/92.

024903   DB731889   ZAV
Allocated to Ditton Creosoting Depot. Scrapped at Ditton Creosoting Depot by Queenborough Railway Materials, Renishaw 4/92.

024913   -   -
Number issued to KDB752868 for use at Speke Sidings, Garston but subsequently cancelled as the vehicle was badly damaged by fire. Now stored awaiting disposal at Liverpool Spekeland Road Freight Depot.

024937   DB985772   ZBO
Allocated to Ditton Creosoting Depot. Scrapped at Ditton Creosoting Depot by Queenborough Railway Materials, Renishaw 4/92.

024938   DB986016   ZBO
Allocated to Ditton Creosoting Depot. Scrapped at Ditton Creosoting Depot by Queenborough Railway Materials, Renishaw 4/92.

024939   DB985887   ZBO
Allocated to Ditton Creosoting Depot. Scrapped at Ditton Creosoting Depot by Queenborough Railway Materials, Renishaw 4/92.

024940   DB984168   ZBO
Allocated to Ditton Creosoting Depot. Scrapped at Ditton Creosoting Depot by Queenborough Railway Materials, Renishaw 4/92.

024941   DB985536   ZBO
Allocated to Ditton Creosoting Depot. Scrapped at Ditton Creosoting Depot by Queenborough Railway Materials, Renishaw 4/92.

024942   DB985794   ZBO
Allocated to Ditton Creosoting Depot. Scrapped at Ditton Creosoting Depot by Queenborough Railway Materials, Renishaw 4/92.

024943   -   -
Number issued to DB985290 for use at Ditton Creosoting Depot, but subsequently cancelled, the vehicle instead being scrapped at Coopers Metals, Handsworth 9/91.

024944   -   -
Number issued to DB984121 for use at Ditton Creosoting Depot, but subsequently cancelled, the vehicle instead being scrapped at Coopers Metals, Handsworth 9/91.

024945   -   -
Number issued to DB986122 for use at Ditton Creosoting Depot, but subsequently cancelled, the vehicle instead being scrapped at Coopers Metals, Handsworth 9/91.

024946   -   -
Number issued to DB990923 for use at Ditton Creosoting Depot, but subsequently cancelled, the vehicle instead being sold to Coopers Metals, Handsworth for scrap.

024947   -   -
Number issued to DB985131 for use at Ditton Creosoting Depot, but subsequently cancelled, the vehicle instead being scrapped at Coopers Metals, Handsworth 8/91.

024948   -   -
Number issued to DB986062 for use at Ditton Creosoting Depot, but subsequently cancelled, the vehicle instead being scrapped at Coopers Metals, Handsworth 8/91.

024954   -   -
Number issued to 93533 for use at Derby Etches Park T&RSMD, but subsequently cancelled, the vehicle having already been acquired by the Crewe Heritage Centre.

024971   -   -
Number issued to KDB977140 for use at Crewe Gresty Road S&T Yard but subsequently cancelled, the vehicle having already been acquired by the Crewe Heritage Centre.

EASTERN REGION – 04XXXX

Allocated numbers have reached 042207. The number series began in July 1950 with 040000 and has been used consecutively ever since. Also included at the end of the current stock are the only three survivors from the former NER 04XXXX fleet.

Current Stock

No.	Former Identity	Carkind	Location
041182	B904546	XLV	BREL York
041183	B904551	XLV	BREL York
041185	B753473	VVV	British Steel, Lackenby
041186	B851790	VSV	British Steel, Lackenby
041203	SHELL A3282	ZRO	Tinsley Yard
041204	SHELL A444	ZRO	Tinsley TMD
041207	DW27038	ZGO	Beighton EY
041208	TDW112869	ZRV	Tinsley TMD
041213	DM574586	ZAV	Tinsley Yard
041227	W116695	VVV	Tilbury Riverside
041244	DW125956	ZRV	Connington Tip – grounded
041249	108	Loco Tender	Thornaby TMD
041252	E281984	OHV	Tinsley Yard
041253	E750340	VVV	Norwich Thorpe Yard
041279	ESSO1873	ZRO	Holbeck TMD
041280	ESSO2716	ZRO	Thornaby TMD
041281	B737914	FAV	BREL York
041282	B709314	FAV	BREL York
041291	W123587	VVV	Norwich Thorpe Yard
041293	CDB916746	ZDV	BREL York
041294	ADB998509	ZSV	Tinsley Yard
041295	ADB998510	ZSV	Tinsley Yard
041306	ADE320838	QXV	Ilford T&RSMD
041311	B850489	VSV	Ipswich Station
041317	TDB975355	QRV	Norwich Crown Point T&RSMD
041321	TDB975359	QRV	Norwich Thorpe Yard
041327	TDM975092	QSV	Tyneside Central Freight Depot – Car Unloading Dock
041329 *	B748668	FVV	Harwich Town Station
041333	B506156	FAV	Tyneside Central Freight Depot
041334	B503045	FAV	Tyneside Central Freight Depot
041339	ADW44012	ZRV	Thornaby TMD – grounded
041344 *	E1308	NOV	BRML Doncaster
041348	ADW2960	ZRV	Immingham TMD
041349	M730840	CAO	North Walsham
041351 *	B941239	BDV	BREL York
041356	ADW3018	ZRV	Ferme Park CS
041357 *	ADW2016	ZRV	Immingham TMD
041358	W2506	CMV	Hornsey Up CS
041361	B749750	ZRV	Gateshead
041363	B889139	Bocar	Harwich Town Station
041364	DM730093	ZTO	Hoveton and Wroxham
041369	E65604	DTSO	Ilford T&RSMD
041379 *	DM395951	QRV	York Leeman Road EY
041381	DE900753	YAO	Crofton PW Yard
041384	DE960608	YAO	Crofton PW Yard
041396	DB994512	YBA	Chesterton Junction PW Yard
041397	DB994511	YBA	Chesterton Junction PW Yard
041405	W291	NFV	Tyneside Central Freight Depot

Number	Code	Type	Location
041406	B749751	ZRV	Immingham TMD - off track
041416	B773727	VVV	Leeds Holbeck TMD
041417	B761701	VVV	Tinsley Yard
041420	ADE87318	ZRV	Norwich Thorpe Yard
041421	B872042	VVV	Immingham TMD
041426	W315	NAV	Tyneside Central Freight Depot
041433	B927006	BDV	BREL York
041450 *	ADB952647	ZTO	Neville Hill T&RSMD
041451 *	B118443	MCO	Immingham TMD
041454	TDE295193	ZGV	Tyneside Central Freight Depot
041465 *	B781176	VVV	Norwich Thorpe Yard - grounded
041467 *	S1274	NQV	Chesterton Junction PW Yard - grounded
041474	ADB975418	QRV	Worksop Station Yard - grounded
041475 *	ADW87706	ZRV	Shirebrook FP
041478	B777800	VVV	Cambridge Up Sidings
041479	B765015	VVV	Doncaster Marshgate EY
041480 *	B773706	VVV	Doncaster Marshgate EY
041482	ADB750378	ZDV	Crofton PW Yard
041486	ADB975556	QRV	Hornsey Up CS
041488	DB854906	ZDV	Bounds Green T&RSMD
041498	B786161	VVV	Neville Hill T&RSMD
041499	ADW44000	ZRV	Hornsey Up CS
041502 *	E1371	NOV	BREL York
041508	S203	NFV	RFS Doncaster
041509	B764907	VVV	Whitemoor Yard
041511 *	CDB506211	ZSO	BREL York
041512 *	CDB710066	ZSO	BREL York
041515 *	CDB734425	ZSO	BREL York
041516 *	CDB738886	ZSO	BREL York
041531	DW139505	ZDV	Leyton EY (carries 041260 in error)
041532	KDB786254	ZDV	Doncaster OHLM Depot - grounded (carries 041262 in error)
041534	KDE75100	ZRV	Doncaster Marshgate EY - grounded (carries 041264 in error)
041537	B773400	VVV	Doncaster OHLM Depot - grounded (carries 041267 in error)
041538	B780778	VVV	Doncaster OHLM Depot - grounded (carries 041268 in error)
041539	B786554	VVV	Doncaster OHLM Depot - grounded (carries 041269 in error)
041540	B762398	VVV	Doncaster OHLM Depot - grounded (carries 041270 in error)
041541	M31100	NFV	Wakefield Kirkgate S&T Depot
041542	M31054	NFV	Wakefield Kirkgate S&T Depot
041543	M31376	NFV	Norwich Thorpe Yard
041544	M31047	NFV	Ipswich WRD
041546	M31216	NFV	Wakefield Kirkgate S&T Depot
041557	DB932068	ZDO	Tyne Yard
041558	DB932093	ZDO	Tyne Yard
041562	B229868	MCO	Hornsey Up CS
041563	B264632	MCO	Hornsey Up CS
041570	M80963	NAV	RFS Doncaster
041572	CDE296229	ZGV	BREL York
041573	CDW138497	ZGV	BREL York
041574	CDB725765	ZGV	BREL York
041575	CDS6367	ZGV	BREL York
041577	CDB725774	ZGV	BREL York
041578	CDW132080	ZGV	BREL York
041584	M31333	NFV	Wakefield Kirkgate S&T Depot
041585	M31932	NFV	Wakefield Kirkgate S&T Depot

041587	DB764748	ZDV		Doncaster Wood Yard
041588	DB779898	ZDV		Doncaster Wood Yard
041589	DB775836	ZDV		Doncaster Marshgate EY
041590	DB762037	ZDV		Doncaster Marshgate EY
041591	DB758935	ZDV		Doncaster Marshgate EY
041592 *	DB750504	ZDV		Doncaster Marshgate EY
041595	B778175	VVV		Leyton EY
041596	B762018	VVV		Leyton EY
041597	E80990	NAV		Shirebrook FP
041602	B785609	VVV		Tyne Yard (carries 041562 in error)
041603	B786459	VVV		Tyneside Central Freight Depot (carries 041563 in error)
041604	B755543	VVV		Sunderland South Dock (carries 041564 in error)
041606	E4688	TSO		Hornsey Up CS (carries 041566 in error)
041607	ADB704328	ZXV		Hull Dairycoates WRD
041614	CDS70025	QRV		RFS Doncaster
041618	M31220	NFV		BRML Doncaster
041619	ADB785327	ZRV		BRML Doncaster
041620	ADB770697	ZRV		BRML Doncaster
041621	B785444	VVV		Cambridge Up Sidings
041622	B942667	BDO		Immingham TMD
041626	ADB977002	QRV		Crofton PW Yard - grounded
041627	ADB977003	QRV		Crofton PW Yard - grounded
041634 *	B785217	VVV		Healey Mills Yard - grounded
041635 *	B775648	VVV		Healey Mills Yard - grounded
041638	W94522	NPV		Wakefield Kirkgate S&T Depot
041639	E94496	NPV		Wakefield Kirkgate S&T Depot
041640	E94630	NPV		Wakefield Kirkgate S&T Depot
041641	W94589	NPV		Wakefield Kirkgate S&T Depot
041645	B951027	CAO		Diss
041650	B933535	SPV		South Milford
041651	B934985	SPV		Stratford TMD
041652	B933489	SPV		Stratford TMD
041653	B935727	SPV		Stratford TMD
041655	B782996	VWV		Stratford Market
041656	B783338	VWV		Stratford LIFT
041657	B783494	VWV		Stratford LIFT
041658	B783602	VWV		Stratford LIFT
041659	B783710	VWV		Stratford Market
041660	B783730	VWV		Stratford Market
041661	B784254	VWV		Stratford LIFT
041662	B784262	VWV		Stratford Market
041663	B784296	VWV		Stratford Market
041664	B784305	VWV		Stratford Market
041671	B933248	SPV		Immingham Tor Line FLT
041672	B920370	SPO		Stratford TMD
041673	ADW118718	ZGO		Peterborough Crescent Wharf WRD
041676 *	S94887	NPV		Parkeston Quay Yard - grounded
041680	DB257698	ZHO		Stratford TMD
041681 *	B558090	MCV		Dalgety Franklyn, Kings Lynn Harbour
041682	S1313	NQV		Leyton EY
041683	S1414	NOV		Leyton EY
041684	B952532	CAO		Healey Mills Yard
041693	M94102	NPV		Finsbury Park Stone Yard
041694	E94642	NPV		Finsbury Park Stone Yard
041695	M94122	NPV		Darlington - grounded
041696	M94281	NPV		Darlington - grounded
041697 *	E94486	NPV		BRML Doncaster
041699 *	E94620	NPV		BREL York

041704	B783719	VMV	Tyneside Central Freight Depot
041705	B783734	VMV	Tyneside Central Freight Depot
041706	B784385	VMV	Gateshead WRD
041714	W94525	NPV	Thornaby TMD
041715	LDB944919	YYO	Costain Concrete, Coltness
041716	LDB945024	YYO	Costain Concrete, Coltness
041717	LDB944275	YYO	Costain Concrete, Coltness
041718	LDB922274	YYO	Costain Concrete, Coltness
041719	LDB922123	YYO	Costain Concrete, Coltness
041720	LDB945480	YYO	Costain Concrete, Coltness
041721	ADB975939	QXV	Doncaster TMD - grounded
041722	ADB975942	QXV	Doncaster TMD
041727 *	B931766	SPV	Sunderland South Dock
041728 *	DB935587	ZDV	Sunderland South Dock
041729 *	DB935495	ZDV	Sunderland South Dock
041730 *	DB935465	ZDV	Sunderland South Dock
041733	B783329	VMV	York WRD - grounded
041735	B732272	STV	Tinsley Yard
041738	B933586	SPV	BREL York
041831	DE283710	ZQV	Hitchin OTPD
041836 *	B756006	VVV	Blyth Cambois TMD - grounded
041839	DB904565	ZXQ	Immingham TMD
041840	B931520	SPV	Immingham TMD
041842 *	M94753	NPV	Bounds Green T&RSMD - grounded
041843 *	E94462	NPV	Bounds Green T&RSMD - grounded
041844	KDB975937	QRV	Grantham
041845	KDB975943	QRV	Grantham (carries 081845 in error)
041850	94355	NPV	Thornaby TMD
041851	94574	NPV	Thornaby TMD
041859	TDB769431	ZRV	Thornaby TMD
041860	TDB770327	ZRV	Thornaby TMD (carries 041859 in error)
041861	TDB775810	ZRV	Thornaby TMD (carries 041859 in error)
041862	TDB779881	ZRV	Thornaby TMD (carries 041859 in error)
041865	KDB765636	ZDV	Darlington Park Lane Yard
041866	KDB768358	ZRV	Retford
041867	KDB771392	ZDV	Retford
041868	KDB784652	ZRV	Retford
041871	94657	NPV	Cambridge EY
041872	94825	NPV	Cambridge EY
041873	KDB852699	ZRV	Cambridge EY
041874	KDB853151	ZDV	Cambridge EY
041875	KDB853768	ZRV	Cambridge EY
041876	KDB875409	ZRV	Cambridge EY
041877	KDB875760	ZRV	Cambridge EY
041878	KDB761022	ZDV	Darlington Park Lane Yard
041879	KDB767765	ZDV	Goole Yard
041881	TDB784175	ZRV	Blyth Cambois TMD
041882	ADW44019	ZRV	Thornaby TMD NYMR
041888 *	ADB975449	ZRV	Thornaby TMD
041889 *	B954420	CAO	Hoveton and Wroxham
041890	KDB785828	ZDV	Darlington Park Lane Yard
041896	M31225	NFV	Wakefield Kirkgate S&T Depot
041898	84608	NAV	York Leeman Road EY
041899	80610	NAV	York Leeman Road EY
041900	B947937	FWV	Neville Hill T&RSMD
041901	B510001	FWV	Neville Hill T&RSMD
041902	B947960	FWV	Neville Hill T&RSMD
041904	84271	NAV	York Leeman Road EY
041905	80721	NAV	York Leeman Road EY
041906	B510044	FWV	Romford OHLM Depot

041907	B947860	FWV	Ilford T&RSMD
041908	B947912	FWV	Ilford T&RSMD
041909 *	B510037	FWV	Stratford TMD
041910	B947916	FWV	Stratford TMD
041911	ADB975419	ZVV	Tinsley TMD
041912	ADB977104	QRV	Attercliffe Sidings, Sheffield
041913	ADB977105	QRV	Attercliffe Sidings, Sheffield
041914 *	B934718	RRV	Gateshead WRD
041915	DB994056	YAO	Crofton PW Yard
041916	DB994078	YAO	Crofton PW Yard
041917	DE274559	YAO	Chesterton Junction PW Yard
041918	DE470776	YAO	Chesterton Junction PW Yard
041919 *	DB994010	YAO	Chesterton Junction PW Yard
041920	DB994012	YAO	Chesterton Junction PW Yard
041921	DB994036	YAO	Chesterton Junction PW Yard
041922	DB994071	YAO	Chesterton Junction PW Yard
041923	TDB904641	ZSV	Colchester Yard
041946	93288	NKV	Ilford T&RSMD
041947	93425	NKV	Ilford T&RSMD
041950	KDB761677	ZRV	Gateshead WRD
041951	DB994002	YAO	Costain Concrete, Coltness
041952	DB994006	YAO	Costain Concrete, Coltness
041954	84027	NAV	Ipswich WRD
041955	84085	NAV	Ipswich WRD - grounded
041957	ADE961880	ZRO	Cambridge Up Sidings
041960 *	ADW1985	ZRV	Immingham TMD
041961 *	ADW44018	ZRV	Immingham TMD
041963	ADW44047	ZRV	Doncaster TMD
041964	ADW2996	ZRV	Hull Botanic Gardens DMUD
041966	ADB966601	ZRO	Stratford TMD
041968	ADE180525	ZGV	Langley Green
			(en route to Coopers Metals, Handsworth)
041969	ADB975961	QRV	Ferme Park CS
041970	ADB977064	QRV	Ferme Park CS
041971	ADB784757	ZRV	Ferme Park CS
041972 *	ADB498617	ZXV	Neville Hill T&RSMD
041977 *	ADE321075	ZSP	Thornaby TMD
041978 *	ADE321072	ZSP	Immingham TMD
041979 *	ADS70185	ZSP	Immingham TMD
041981	ADW87973	ZVV	Leyton EY
041982	ADB777837	ZRV	Leyton EY
041983	ADB494471	ZGV	Knottingley TMD
041984	ADB723542	ZGV	Knottingley TMD
041985	ADB558643	ZHV	Knottingley TMD
041986	ADB769566	ZRV	Langley Green
			(en route to Coopers Metals, Handsworth)
041987	ADB764528	ZRV	Langley Green
			(en route to Coopers Metals, Handsworth)
041989	ADB975423	ZRV	Toton Training School
041994	ESSO45110	TSV	Stratford TMD
041995	ESSO45270	TSF	Stratford TMD
041998	ADB530672	ZSQ	BREL York
041999	ADB733500	ZSW	BREL York
042000 *	94899	NPV	Cambridge T&RSMD - grounded
042015	93702	NKV	BRML Doncaster
042016	B333676	HUO	Derbyshire Coalite and Chemical Bolsover
042017	B333779	HUO	Derbyshire Coalite and Chemical Bolsover
042018 *	B333810	HUO	Derbyshire Coalite and Chemical Bolsover
042019	B333826	HUO	Derbyshire Coalite and Chemical Bolsover
042020	B333838	HUO	Derbyshire Coalite and Chemical Bolsover

042021	B333859	HUO	Derbyshire Coalite and Chemical Bolsover
042022	B333869	HUO	Derbyshire Coalite and Chemical Bolsover
042023	B333896	HUO	Derbyshire Coalite and Chemical Bolsover
042024 *	B333897	HUO	Derbyshire Coalite and Chemical Bolsover
042025	B333956	HUO	Derbyshire Coalite and Chemical Bolsover
042026	B334020	HUO	Derbyshire Coalite and Chemical Bolsover
042027	B334039	HUO	Derbyshire Coalite and Chemical Bolsover
042028	B334138	HUO	Derbyshire Coalite and Chemical Bolsover
042029	B334152	HUO	Derbyshire Coalite and Chemical Bolsover
042030	B334155	HUO	Derbyshire Coalite and Chemical Bolsover
042031	B334156	HUO	Derbyshire Coalite and Chemical Bolsover
042032	B334173	HUO	Derbyshire Coalite and Chemical Bolsover
042033 *	B334174	HUO	Derbyshire Coalite and Chemical Bolsover
042034	B334177	HUO	Derbyshire Coalite and Chemical Bolsover
042035	B334204	HUO	Derbyshire Coalite and Chemical Bolsover
042036	B334240	HUO	Derbyshire Coalite and Chemical Bolsover
042037	B334256	HUO	Derbyshire Coalite and Chemical Bolsover
042038	B334305	HUO	Derbyshire Coalite and Chemical Bolsover
042039	B334320	HUO	Derbyshire Coalite and Chemical Bolsover
042040	B334325	HUO	Derbyshire Coalite and Chemical Bolsover
042041	B334396	HUO	Derbyshire Coalite and Chemical Bolsover
042042 *	B334429	HUO	Derbyshire Coalite and Chemical Bolsover
042043	B334501	HUO	Derbyshire Coalite and Chemical Bolsover
042044	B334507	HUO	Derbyshire Coalite and Chemical Bolsover
042045	B334556	HUO	Derbyshire Coalite and Chemical Bolsover
042046	B334569	HUO	Derbyshire Coalite and Chemical Bolsover
042047	B334715	HUO	Derbyshire Coalite and Chemical Bolsover
042049	B334792	HUO	Derbyshire Coalite and Chemical Bolsover
042050	B334842	HUO	Derbyshire Coalite and Chemical Bolsover
042051	B334862	HUO	Derbyshire Coalite and Chemical Bolsover
042052	B334926	HUO	Derbyshire Coalite and Chemical Bolsover
042053	B334989	HUO	Derbyshire Coalite and Chemical Bolsover
042054	B335010	HUO	Derbyshire Coalite and Chemical Bolsover
042055	B335039	HUO	Derbyshire Coalite and Chemical Bolsover
042056	B335079	HUO	Derbyshire Coalite and Chemical Bolsover
042057	B335100	HUO	Derbyshire Coalite and Chemical Bolsover
042058	B335104	HUO	Derbyshire Coalite and Chemical Bolsover
042059	B335152	HUO	Derbyshire Coalite and Chemical Bolsover
042060 *	B335190	HUO	Derbyshire Coalite and Chemical Bolsover
042061	B335229	HUO	Derbyshire Coalite and Chemical Bolsover
042062	B335234	HUO	Derbyshire Coalite and Chemical Bolsover
042063	B335315	HUO	Derbyshire Coalite and Chemical Bolsover
042064	B335485	HUO	Derbyshire Coalite and Chemical Bolsover
042065	B335507	HUO	Derbyshire Coalite and Chemical Bolsover
042066	B335526	HUO	Derbyshire Coalite and Chemical Bolsover
042067	B335537	HUO	Derbyshire Coalite and Chemical Bolsover
042068	B335570	HUO	Derbyshire Coalite and Chemical Bolsover
042069	B335701	HUO	Derbyshire Coalite and Chemical Bolsover
042070	B335789	HUO	Derbyshire Coalite and Chemical Bolsover
042071	B335817	HUO	Derbyshire Coalite and Chemical Bolsover
042072	B335828	HUO	Derbyshire Coalite and Chemical Bolsover
042073	B335851	HUO	Derbyshire Coalite and Chemical Bolsover
042074	B335853	HUO	Derbyshire Coalite and Chemical Bolsover
042075	B335860	HUO	Derbyshire Coalite and Chemical Bolsover
042076	B335892	HUO	Derbyshire Coalite and Chemical Bolsover
042077	B335898	HUO	Derbyshire Coalite and Chemical Bolsover
042078 *	B335957	HUO	Derbyshire Coalite and Chemical Bolsover
042079	B335975	HUO	Derbyshire Coalite and Chemical Bolsover
042080	B336095	HUO	Derbyshire Coalite and Chemical Bolsover
042081	B336109	HUO	Derbyshire Coalite and Chemical Bolsover

042082 *	B336198	HUO	Derbyshire Coalite and Chemical Bolsover
042083	B336390	HUO	Derbyshire Coalite and Chemical Bolsover
042084	B336465	HUO	Derbyshire Coalite and Chemical Bolsover
042085	B336539	HUO	Derbyshire Coalite and Chemical Bolsover
042086	B336542	HUO	Derbyshire Coalite and Chemical Bolsover
042087	B336558	HUO	Derbyshire Coalite and Chemical Bolsover
042088	B336569	HUO	Derbyshire Coalite and Chemical Bolsover
042089	B336616	HUO	Derbyshire Coalite and Chemical Bolsover
042090	B336769	HUO	Derbyshire Coalite and Chemical Bolsover
042091	B336792	HUO	Derbyshire Coalite and Chemical Bolsover
042092	B336803	HUO	Derbyshire Coalite and Chemical Bolsover
042093	B336821	HUO	Derbyshire Coalite and Chemical Bolsover
042094	B336830	HUO	Derbyshire Coalite and Chemical Bolsover
042095	B336847	HUO	Derbyshire Coalite and Chemical Bolsover
042096	B336861	HUO	Derbyshire Coalite and Chemical Bolsover
042097	B336908	HUO	Derbyshire Coalite and Chemical Bolsover
042098	B336937	HUO	Derbyshire Coalite and Chemical Bolsover
042099 *	B336966	HUO	Derbyshire Coalite and Chemical Bolsover
042100	B337043	HUO	Derbyshire Coalite and Chemical Bolsover
042101	B337052	HUO	Derbyshire Coalite and Chemical Bolsover
042102	B337110	HUO	Derbyshire Coalite and Chemical Bolsover
042103	B337166	HUO	Derbyshire Coalite and Chemical Bolsover
042104	B337190	HUO	Derbyshire Coalite and Chemical Bolsover
042105	B337276	HUO	Derbyshire Coalite and Chemical Bolsover
042106	B337300	HUO	Derbyshire Coalite and Chemical Bolsover
042107	B337306	HUO	Derbyshire Coalite and Chemical Bolsover
042108	B337328	HUO	Derbyshire Coalite and Chemical Bolsover
042109	B337343	HUO	Derbyshire Coalite and Chemical Bolsover
042110	B337385	HUO	Derbyshire Coalite and Chemical Bolsover
042111	B337405	HUO	Derbyshire Coalite and Chemical Bolsover
042112	B337525	HUO	Derbyshire Coalite and Chemical Bolsover
042113	B337533	HUO	Derbyshire Coalite and Chemical Bolsover
042114	B337593	HUO	Derbyshire Coalite and Chemical Bolsover
042115	B337693	HUO	Derbyshire Coalite and Chemical Bolsover
042116	B337742	HUO	Derbyshire Coalite and Chemical Bolsover
042117	B337825	HUO	Derbyshire Coalite and Chemical Bolsover
042118	B337896	HUO	Derbyshire Coalite and Chemical Bolsover
042119 *	B337923	HUO	Derbyshire Coalite and Chemical Bolsover
042120	B337946	HUO	Derbyshire Coalite and Chemical Bolsover
042121	B338085	HUO	Derbyshire Coalite and Chemical Bolsover
042122	B338088	HUO	Derbyshire Coalite and Chemical Bolsover
042123 *	B338118	HUO	Derbyshire Coalite and Chemical Bolsover
042126	93828	NKV	Tinsley TMD
042128 *	ADB909007	YVP	BRML Doncaster
042129	ADB909012	YVP	BRML Doncaster
042130	KDB779978	ZRV	Kings Lynn Station Yard
042131	B950464	CAO	Whitemoor Yard
042133	84168	NAV	Heaton T&RSMD
042134	84199	NAV	Heaton T&RSMD
042135	93213	NKV	Heaton T&RSMD
042141	KDB772630	ZRV	Norwich Thorpe Yard
042142 *	DB994112	YBO	Chesterton Junction PW Yard
042143 *	DB994210	YBO	Chesterton Junction PW Yard
042144 *	DB994221	YBO	Chesterton Junction PW Yard
042145	DB996340	YMO	Crofton PW Yard
042146	DB994609	YBO	Crofton PW Yard
042147	84003	NCV	Cambridge T&RSMD
042148	80638	NAV	Ilford T&RSMD
042149	KDB784802	ZRV	Ipswich WRD
042150	ADB999067	ZRF	Stratford TMD

042151	ADB999048	ZRF	Stratford TMD
042152	DB946057	YNP	York WRD
042153	DB946060	YNP	York WRD
042154	93975	NKV	Ipswich Upper Yard
042155	ADB999050	ZRW	Toton Training School
042156	DB452545	ZSV	Beighton EY
042157	DB917363	ZSO	Beighton EY
042158 *	200646	VBA	Doncaster Belmont Yard - grounded
042159	DB990321	ZBO	Crofton PW Yard
042160	DB986196	ZBO	Crofton PW Yard
042161	DB986508	ZBO	Crofton PW Yard
042162	DB984782	ZBO	Crofton PW Yard
042163	DB986054	ZBO	Crofton PW Yard
042164	DB554854	ZHV	Crofton PW Yard
042165	DB994041	YAO	Crofton PW Yard
042166	DB994622	YBO	Crofton PW Yard
042167 *	TDB904529	ZVV	Tinsley TMD
042168	200250	VBA	Thornaby TMD
042169	200251	VBA	Thornaby TMD
042170	200302	VBA	Thornaby TMD
042171	200551	VBA	Thornaby TMD
042172	200586	VBA	Thornaby TMD
042173	200610	VBA	Thornaby TMD
042174	ADB999026	ZRW	Tinsley TMD
042175	ADB999063	ZRW	Sheffield Station
042176 *	DE470820	ZPO	Doncaster Wood Yard
042177 *	ADB701441	ZRV	Colchester Yard
042178 *	DB990435	ZBO	Colchester Yard
042179	80526	NAV	Norwich Crown Point T&RSMD - grounded
042180	ESS066230	TTA	Neville Hill T&RSMD
042181	ESS066214	TTA	Neville Hill T&RSMD
042182	ESS066319	TTA	Blyth Cambois TMD
042183 *	ESS066207	TTA	Heaton T&RSMD
042184 *	ESS066326	TTA	Heaton T&RSMD
042185	ESS066316	TTA	Immingham TMD
042186	ESS066233	TTA	Norwich Crown Point T&RSMD
042187	DB889020	ZXX	Morpeth
042188	93831	NKV	York WRD
042189 *	210386	VDA	Rotherham Masborough Steel Terminal
042190	ADB321088	QQV	Knottingley TMD
042191	ADB749673	ZRQ	Stratford TMD
042192	ADB999071	ZRW	Stratford TMD
042193 *	ADB999061	ZRW	Heaton T&RSMD
042194	ADB999072	ZRW	Ripple Lane SD
042195	ADB999075	ZRW	Frodingham SD
042196	ADB999077	ZRW	Blyth Cambois TMD
042197	DB768924	ZDV	Doncaster Wood Yard
042198 *	ADB999022	ZRW	Knottingley TMD
042199 *	ADB999023	ZRW	Knottingley TMD
042200	ADB999060	ZRW	Hull Botanic Gardens TMD
042201 *	ADB999064	ZRG	Hull Botanic Gardens TMD
042202 *	ADB999070	ZRW	Hull Botanic Gardens TMD
042203	200753	VDA	Doncaster Station
042204 *	400042	FBA	Tinsley TMD
042205 *	DM45030	QXA	York WRD
042206 *	ADB975329	ZVV	Frodingham SD
042207 *	ADB577004	ZHV	Cambridge T&RSMD

042227 TE   042239 NC   042232 TE   3381 HE
042217 T1 (DB110638)   042226 TE   042240 TE   6360 NL
042220 IPSWICH S+T   042245 TE   042222 NL
042223 IPSWICH S+T
042234 IL   042241 TE
042243 T1

041568 is pictured at Immingham Dock on 7th September 1986. Despite being severely fire damaged this 1927 built coach was purchased for preservation in order that its underframe and bogies could be used with ECJS Dining Car No. 189.   Bob Wallace

Originally NPV 94493 and latterly stores van ADB977002, 041626 is pictured at Crofton PW Yard on 27th August 1980. The majority of vehicles grounded for use as stores are not allocated internal user numbers, 041626/7 at Crofton being two of the exceptions.   Brian Cuttell

GWR 5.5 plank open wagon ADW118718, pictured here as 041673 at Peterborough Crescent Wharf WRD on 6th October 1985, is bound to attract interest from the preservation movement when it eventually is made available for disposal. Bob Wallace

One of the last BR internal users to be found on a dock railway system is 060962, pictured here in Newport Docks on 12th June 1989. Deryck W. Lewis

Former NER Series

042099	B23785	-	BREL York
042431	DW112884	ZRV	Thirsk
042468	E9291	BSO	Thornaby TMD

Vehicles No Longer In Stock

No.   Former Identity   Carkind

041500   M87727   NRV
Allocated to Doncaster Works. Grounded. Scrapped at Doncaster Works during the latter half of 1987.

041501   E70505   NFV
Allocated to York Works. Sold from York Works to Sea Containers 1/84 and broken up for spares at Steamtown, Carnforth during 1984.

041503   S1370   NQV
Allocated to Doncaster Works. Scrapped at Doncaster Works by Rollason, Telford 4/89.

041504   ADE87358   ZRV
Allocated to York Clifton CS. Scrapped at Marple and Gillott, Sheffield 8/85.

041505   ADW123385   ZRV
Allocated to York Clifton CS. Scrapped at Marple and Gillott, Sheffield 8/85.

041506   M31915   NFV
Allocated to Kings Lynn. Later Lincoln. Scrapped at Coopers Metals, Sheffield 12/82.

041507   ADW124264   ZRO
Allocated to York Clifton CS. Scrapped at Marple and Gillott, Sheffield 8/85.

041510   S209   NFV
Allocated to Doncaster Works. Grounded. Scrapped at Doncaster Works during the latter half of 1987.

041513   -   -
Number issued to CDB733500 but subsequently cancelled. See 041999.

041514   CDB733762   ZSV
Allocated to York Works. Believed scrapped at York Works during 1988.

041517   CDB916885   ZSO
Allocated to Doncaster Works and coupled to diesel-mechanical crane 55095 (later ADRT96031 when transferred to Doncaster Carr). Scrapped at Doncaster Carr by Lincoln Ferrous Metals, Lincoln 10/88.

041518   CDM306100   ZSO
Allocated to Doncaster Works and coupled to diesel-mechanical crane 55095 (later ADRT96031 when transferred to Doncaster Carr). Scrapped at Doncaster Carr by Lincoln Ferrous Metals, Lincoln 10/88.

041519   CDM501035   ZRV
Allocated to Doncaster Works. Originally allocated 041443. Scrapped at Doncaster Works by Lincoln Ferrous Metals, Lincoln 1/89.

041520   CDS65196   ZRV
Allocated to Doncaster Works. Originally allocated 041439.   Scrapped at Doncaster Works during 1987.

041521   CDW142393   ZRV
Allocated to Doncaster Works. Originally allocated 041442.   Scrapped at Doncaster Works during 1986.

041522   CDM725501   ZVO
Allocated to Doncaster Works. Originally allocated 041441.   Scrapped at Doncaster Works by Lincoln Ferrous Metals, Lincoln 1/89.

041523   -   -
Number issued to CDM522090 for use at Doncaster Works but subsequently cancelled the vehicle having already been scrapped. Originally allocated 041440.

041524   -   -
Number issued to CDM700601 for use at Doncaster Works but subsequently cancelled the vehicle having already been scrapped.

041525   KDS65863   ZRV
Allocated to Darlington. Scrapped at Darlington during 1984.

041526   E21095   BCK
Allocated to Heaton T&RSMD. Scrapped at Booth Roe Metals, Rotherham 3/92.

041527   B930504   SPO
Allocated to Lincoln. Scrapped at Coopers Metals, Sheffield 8/82.

041528   B931109   SPO
Allocated to Lincoln. Scrapped at Coopers Metals, Sheffield 8/82.

041529   B945215   BCO   (Issued in error as 041259)
Allocated to Ripple Lane WRD. Scrapped at Ripple Lane WRD by Steel Supply, Barking 11/81.

041530   DE455305   ZDO   (Issued in error as 041260)
Allocated to Leyton Engineers Yard. Scrapped at Leyton Engineers Yard by Morris, Romford 2/87.

041533   KDB881772   ZRV   (Issued in error as 041263)
Allocated to Grantham. Scrapped at Grantham by Ward Ferrous Metals, Chepstow 3/91.

041535   KDE632438   ZPO   (Issued in error as 041265)
Allocated to Wakefield Withams Sidings. Scrapped at Wakefield Withams Sidings by Cartwright, Tipton 6/82.

041536   KDM196637   ZQV   (Issued in error as 041266)
Allocated to Wakefield Withams Sidings. Scrapped at Wakefield Withams Sidings by Cartwright, Tipton 6/82.

041545   M31227   NFV
Allocated to Huddersfield. Scrapped at Huddersfield by Vic Berry, Leicester 4/90.

041547   B483482   OHO
Allocated to BREL Temple Mills Wagon Works. Scrapped at Temple Mills Yard by Goldpawn, Swansea 7/84.

041548   B496997   OHO
Allocated to BREL Temple Mills Wagon Works. Scrapped at Temple Mills Yard by Goldpawn, Swansea 7/84.

041549   B494043   OHO
Allocated to BREL Temple Mills Wagon Works. Believed scrapped at Temple Mills Wagon Works during 1983.

041550   B495316   OHO
Allocated to BREL Temple Mills Wagon Works. Scrapped at Temple Mills Yard by Goldpawn, Swansea 7/84.

041551   S2125   NQV
Allocated to Doncaster Works. Scrapped at Doncaster Works by Maize Metals, Wednesbury 6/90.

041552   ADB975656   QRV
Allocated to Doncaster Works. Scrapped at Doncaster Works by Higgs, Barnsley 3/91.

041553   ADW2838   ZRV
Allocated to Colchester. Scrapped at Marple and Gillott, Sheffield 11/87.

041554   TDE321100   ZSV
Allocated to Doncaster Works, Later Doncaster Carr. Sold from Doncaster Carr to the Keighley and Worth Valley Railway 5/92.

041555   B935497   SPV
Allocated to Tinsley TMD. Scrapped at Booth Roe Metals, Rotherham 3/88.

041556   E292328   SPV
Allocated to Goole. Scrapped at Goole during 1990.

041559   -   -
Number issued to a ZDO (no specific vehicle selected) for use at Tyne Yard but subsequently cancelled.

041560   -   -
Number issued to a ZDO (no specific vehicle selected) for use at Tyne Yard but subsequently cancelled.

041561   B785736   VVV
Allocated to Hitchin CE Stockyard. Scrapped at Hitchin CE Stockyard by Lincoln Ferrous Metals, Lincoln 3/90.

041564   B952747   CAO
Allocated to Marshmoor Sidings, Hatfield. Scrapped at Steel Breaking and Dismantling, Chesterfield 3/83.

041565   -   -
Number issued to a ZRV (an ex-Western Region milk tank although no specific vehicle selected) for use at Norwich Wensum but subsequently cancelled.

041566   DE141280   ZQO
Allocated to Darlington. Scrapped at Jolly, Darlington 6/81.

041567   S247   NFV
Allocated to Crofton PW Yard. Grounded. Scrapped at Crofton PW Yard during the first half of 1989.

041568   DE320889   QPV
Allocated to Immingham Dock. Badly damaged by fire. Underframe and bogies sold to M. Ford, Hulme on Spalding Moor, York (for use with ECJS Dining Car No. 189) 9/91.

041569   B931656   SPV
Allocated to Healey Mills TMD. Scrapped at Healey Mills TMD by Higgs, Barnsley 10/87.

041571   -   -
Number issued to CDM422184 for use at York Works but subsequently cancelled, the vehicle instead being scrapped at BRML Springburn 11/89.

041576   -   -
Number issued to CDB484044 for use at York Works but subsequently cancelled, the vehicle instead being scrapped at Jolly, Darlington 7/82.

041579   -   -
Number issued to CDB461421 for use at York Works but subsequently cancelled, the vehicle instead being scrapped at Booth, Rotherham 7/82.

041580   S94550   NPV
Allocated to Scarborough. Scrapped at Scarborough by Cartwright, Tipton 4/85.

041581   B780047   VVV
Allocated to York Clifton CS. Scrapped at Marple and Gillott, Sheffield 8/85.

041582   B780313   VVV
Allocated to York Clifton CS. Scrapped at Marple and Gillott, Sheffield 8/85.

041583   M31112   NFV
Allocated to Huddersfield. Scrapped at Huddersfield by Vic Berry, Leicester 4/90.

041586   -   -
Number issued to M31225 but subsequently cancelled. See 041896.

041593   DE321089   QPV
Allocated to Boston. Sold to W. Hall at Swineshead Bridge in 1988. Resold to Stoneyford Lodge Hotel, near Heanor in 1991.

041594   -   -
Number issued to S1806 (NQV) for use at Thornton Fields CS but subsequently cancelled, the vehicle instead being scrapped at Romford by Morris, Romford 10/83.

041598   B780906   VVV
Allocated to Middlesborough Goods Depot. Scrapped at BREL Shildon 10/83.

041599   B772329   VVV
Allocated to Middlesborough Goods Depot. Scrapped at BREL Shildon 10/83.

041600   B780114   VVV   (Issued in error as 041560)
Allocated to Middlesborough Goods Depot. Scrapped at BREL Shildon 10/83.

041601   B780425   VVV   (Issued in error as 041561)
Allocated to Middlesborough Goods Depot. Scrapped at BREL Shildon 10/83.

041605   E21219   BCK
Allocated to Bounds Green T&RSMD. Scrapped at Booth, Rotherham during 1986.

041608   B930707   SPO
Allocated to March TMD. Scrapped at March TMD by Miller, Downham Market 9/91.

041609   -   -
Number issued to B930420 for use at Tyneside Central FD but subsequently cancelled the vehicle having already been scrapped.

041610   B453117   OLV
Allocated to Gainsborough Central. Scrapped at Marple and Gillott, Sheffield 6/84.

041611   B933413   RRV
Allocated to Grimsby Hollies Street FD. Sold from Grimsby Hollies Street FD to the Fulstow Steam Centre, Fulstow near Louth (for use with GER Coach No. 352) during the latter part of 1989.

041612   M80557   NAV
Allocated to Doncaster Works. Scrapped at Doncaster Works by Maize Metals, Wednesbury 6/90.

041613   M81446   NAV
Allocated to Healey Mills TMD. Later York Clifton CS. Scrapped at York WRD by Maize Metals, Wednesbury 12/88.

041615   B772431   VVV
Allocated to Hull Dairycoates WRD. Scrapped at Booth, Rotherham 6/87.

041616   B931678   SPV
Allocated to Tinsley TMD. Sent for scrap to Booth Roe Metals, Rotherham 3/88.

041617   B775831   VVV
Allocated to Hull Botanic Gardens. Scrapped at Roe Bros, Sheffield 7/85.

041623   E80641   NAV
Allocated to York Works. Scrapped at Booth Roe Metals, Rotherham 11/88.

041624   E80568   NAV
Allocated to York Works. Scrapped at Booth Roe Metals, Rotherham 11/88.

041625   M80770   NAV
Allocated to York Works. Scrapped at Booth Roe Metals, Rotherham 11/88.

041628   ADB977004   QRV
Allocated to Dinsdale Long-welded Rail Depot. Grounded. Scrapped at Dinsdale Long-welded Rail Depot during 1991.

041629   ADB977005   QRV
Allocated to Dinsdale Long-welded Rail Depot. Grounded. Scrapped at Dinsdale Long-welded Rail Depot during 1991.

041630   -   -
Number issued to DB982095 for use at Peterborough East Stockyard but subsequently cancelled, the vehicle instead being scrapped at Marple and Gillott, Sheffield 7/84.

041631   B259981   MCO
Allocated to Leeds Holbeck TMD. Scrapped at Marple and Gillott, Sheffield 7/84.

041632   B215669   MCO
Allocated to Leeds Holbeck TMD. Scrapped at Marple and Gillott, Sheffield 7/84.

041633   -   -
Number issued to ADB496817 for use at Leeds Holbeck TMD but subsequently cancelled, the vehicle instead being retained for departmental use in the Leeds area. See 041972.

041636   E80846   NAV
Allocated to York Works. Scrapped at Booth Roe Metals, Rotherham 11/88.

041637   M81058   NAV
Allocated to York Works. Scrapped at Booth Roe Metals, Rotherham 11/88.

041642   E4576   TSO
Allocated to Shildon Wagon Works. Scrapped at Shildon Wagon Works during the latter part of 1984.

041643   E4490   TSO
Allocated to Shildon Wagon Works. Scrapped at Shildon Wagon Works during the latter part of 1984.

041644   M94388   NPV
Allocated to March TMD. Sold from March TMD to D. Wells, Haverhill 7/88.

041646   CDB887027   ZRV
Allocated to Doncaster Works. Scrapped at Doncaster Works by Lincoln Ferrous Metals, Lincoln 1/89.

041647   CDM701047   ZRV
Allocated to Doncaster Works. Scrapped at Doncaster Works by Lincoln Ferrous Metals, Lincoln 1/89.

041648   B796623   VVV
Allocated to Darlington Park Lane. Believed scrapped at Shildon Wagon Works 6/84.

041649   B772583   VVV
Allocated to Darlington Park Lane. Scrapped at Shildon Wagon Works 6/84.

041654   -   -
Number issued to B922991 for use at Sheffield Freight Terminal but subsequently cancelled, the vehicle instead being scrapped at Coopers Metals, Sheffield 2/83.

041665   M80558   NAV
Allocated to Shildon Wagon Works. Scrapped at Shildon Wagon Works during the latter part of 1984.

041666   E4865   TSO
Allocated to Shildon Wagon Works. Scrapped at Shildon Wagon Works during the latter part of 1984.

041667   M94305   NPV
Allocated to Dinsdale Long-welded Rail Depot. Grounded. Scrapped at Dinsdale Long-welded Rail Depot during 1991.

041668   B783291   VWV
Allocated to Hull Dairycoates WRD. Later Hull Botanic Gardens TMD. Scrapped at Hull Hessle Yard by Ward Ferrous Metals, Chepstow 12/89.

041669   B783595   VWV
Allocated to Hull Dairycoates WRD. Later Hull Botanic Gardens TMD. Scrapped at Hull Hessle Yard by Ward Ferrous Metals, Chepstow 12/89.

041670   B782899   VWV
Allocated to Hull Dairycoates WRD. Later Hull Botanic Gardens TMD. Scrapped at Hull Hessle Yard by Ward Ferrous Metals, Chepstow 12/89.

041674   E4296   TSO
Allocated to Stratford TMD. Scrapped at Vic Berry, Leicester 11/85.

041675   E4408   TSO
Allocated to Stratford TMD. Scrapped at Vic Berry, Leicester 11/85.

041677   B787023   RBV
Allocated to Doncaster Works. Scrapped at Doncaster Works by Higgs, Barnsley 2/90.

041678   S1488   NQV
Allocated to Doncaster Works. Scrapped at Doncaster Works by Maize Metals, Wednesbury 6/90.

041679   -   -
Number issued to E94486 but subsequently cancelled. See 041697.

041685   -   -
Number issued to KDB772516 but subsequently cancelled. See 041855.

041686   KDB761037   ZDV
Allocated to York Leeman Road EY. Scrapped at York Leeman Road by BR 8/85.

041687   B732745   STV
Allocated to Ilford T&RSMD. Scrapped at Roe Bros, Sheffield 9/86.

041688   B730825   STV
Allocated to Ilford T&RSMD. Scrapped at Roe Bros, Sheffield 9/86.

041689   B784468   VMV
Allocated to Tyneside Central FD. Scrapped at Tyneside Central FD by Seagrave, West Auckland 11/85.

041690   B784183   VMV
Allocated to Tyneside Central FD. Scrapped at Tyneside Central FD by Seagrave, West Auckland 11/85.

041691   -   -
Number issued to B922544 for use at Dinsdale Long-welded Rail Depot but subsequently cancelled, the vehicle now being in departmental use as LDB922544 at Doncaster Hexthorpe ECD.

041692   -   -
Number issued to M94753 but subsequently cancelled. See 041842.

041698   E94456   NPV
Allocated to York Works. Scrapped at Booth Roe Metals, Rotherham 11/88.

041700   -   -
Number issued to W94539 but subsequently cancelled. See 041852.

041701   W94552   NPV
Allocated to York Works. Scrapped at Bird, Long Marston 9/84.

041702   -   -
Number issued to W94592 but subsequently cancelled. See 041853.

041703   -   -
Number issued to E94646 but subsequently cancelled. See 041854.

041707   DB988525   ZBV
Allocated to Lowestoft CE Harbour Works. Originally allocated 041399. Previously a power unit of a viaduct inspection unit and fitted with a Ford six cylinder diesel engine, this vehicle was regarded as BR's most unusual shunter. Believed scrapped at Lowestoft CE Harbour Works by BR 4/88.

041708   -   -
Number issued to B411414 for use at Thames Haven but subsequently cancelled, the vehicle instead being scrapped by BR at Thames Haven 7/84.

041709   B429730   HTO
Allocated to Thames Haven. Scrapped at Marple and Gillott, Sheffield 7/86.

041710   E289616   HTO
Allocated to Thames Haven. Scrapped at Marple and Gillott, Sheffield 7/86.

041711   E305939   HTO
Allocated to Thames Haven. Scrapped at Marple and Gillott, Sheffield 7/86.

041712   E306659   HTO
Allocated to Thames Haven. Scrapped at Marple and Gillott, Sheffield 7/86.

041713   E306684   HTO
Allocated to Thames Haven. Scrapped at Marple and Gillott, Sheffield 7/86.

041723   -   -
Number issued to DB975800 but subsequently cancelled. See 041731.

041724   DM473228   ZRV
Allocated to Crofton PW Yard. Scrapped at Crofton PW Yard by Heselwood, Sheffield 6/88.

041725   DB460472   ZRV
Allocated to Crofton PW Yard. Scrapped at Crofton PW Yard by Heselwood, Sheffield 6/88.

041726   DM309065   ZSO
Allocated to Crofton PW Yard. Scrapped at Crofton PW Yard by Heselwood, Sheffield 6/88.

041731   DB975800   QPV
Allocated to Leyton Engineers Yard. Scrapped at Marple and Gillott, Sheffield 4/86.

041732   ADE320919   QXV
Allocated to Wakefield WRD. Scrapped at Coopers Metals, Sheffield 9/85.

041734   B730560   STV
Allocated to Ilford T&RSMD. Scrapped at Coopers Metals, Sheffield 2/91.

041736   B783309   VMV
Allocated to Doncaster Works. Believed scrapped at a Sheffield area scrapyard 11/85.

041737   B932952   SPV
Allocated to Tinsley TMD. Scrapped at Booth Roe Metals, Rotherham 4/88.

041739   B922502   BQV
Allocated to Sheffield Freight Terminal. Returned to Capital Stock as a BCV in 1986. Sold to British Steel, Ravenscraig 8/88.

041740   B922522   BQV
Allocated to Sheffield Freight Terminal.   Scrapped at Coopers Metals, Sheffield 1/86.

041741   B922533   BQV
Allocated to Sheffield Freight Terminal.   Scrapped at Coopers Metals, Sheffield 7/91.

041742   B922535   BQV
Allocated to Sheffield Freight Terminal. Scrapped at Roe Bros, Sheffield 4/86.

041743   B922538   BQV
Allocated to Sheffield Freight Terminal. Returned to Capital Stock as a BCV in 1986. Sold to British Steel, Ravenscraig 8/88.

041744   B922556   BQV
Allocated to Sheffield Freight Terminal. Scrapped at Roe Bros, Sheffield 5/86.

041745   B922568   BQV
Allocated to Sheffield Freight Terminal. Returned to Capital Stock as aBCV in 1986. Allocated to British Steel, Shelton as 024723 5/87.

041746   -   -
Number issued to B922580 for use at Sheffield Freight Terminal but subsequently cancelled, the vehicle instead being scrapped at Coopers Metals, Handsworth 12/84.

041747   B922633   BQV
Allocated to Sheffield Freight Terminal.   Scrapped at Coopers Metals, Sheffield 12/85.

041748   B922639   BQV
Allocated to Sheffield Freight Terminal. Scrapped at Roe Bros, Sheffield 5/86.

041749   B922655   BQV
Allocated to Sheffield Freight Terminal. Scrapped at Roe Bros, Sheffield 5/86.

041750   B922683   BQV
Allocated to Sheffield Freight Terminal.   Scrapped at Coopers Metals, Sheffield 12/85.

041751   B922735   BQV
Allocated to Sheffield Freight Terminal. Returned to Capital Stock as a BCV in 1986. Sold to British Steel, Workington 7/90.

041752   B922763   BQV
Allocated to Sheffield Freight Terminal.   Scrapped at Coopers Metals, Sheffield 1/86.

041753   B922774   BQV
Allocated to Sheffield Freight Terminal.   Scrapped at Coopers Metals, Sheffield 12/85.

041754   B922783   BQV
Allocated to Sheffield Freight Terminal. Returned to Capital Stock as a BCV in 1986. Scrapped at Marple and Gillott, Sheffield 3/89.

041755   B922788   BQV
Allocated to Sheffield Freight Terminal.   Scrapped at Coopers Metals, Sheffield 12/85.

041756   B922806   BQV
Allocated to Sheffield Freight Terminal. Returned to Capital Stock as a BCV in 1986. Sold to British Steel, Workington 7/90.

041757   B922810   BQV
Allocated to Sheffield Freight Terminal. Returned to Capital Stock as a BCV in 1986. Scrapped at Marple and Gillott, Sheffield 3/89.

041758   B922852   BQV
Allocated to Sheffield Freight Terminal. Scrapped at Roe Bros, Sheffield 5/86.

041759   B922853   BQV
Allocated to Sheffield Freight Terminal. Scrapped at Coopers Metals, Sheffield 12/85.

041760   B922869   BQV
Allocated to Sheffield Freight Terminal. Returned to Capital Stock as a BCV in 1986. Sold to British Steel, Workington 7/90.

041761   B922871   BQV
Allocated to Sheffield Freight Terminal. Returned to Capital Stock as a BCV in 1986. Sold to British Steel, Workington 7/90.

041762   B922902   BQV
Allocated to Sheffield Freight Terminal. Returned to Departmental Stock as crane runner LDB922902. Scrapped at Marple and Gillott, Sheffield 11/88.

041763   B922903   BQV
Allocated to Sheffield Freight Terminal. Scrapped at Coopers Metals, Sheffield 12/85.

041764   B922926   BQV
Allocated to Sheffield Freight Terminal. Scrapped at Booth, Rotherham 2/86.

041765   B922942   BQV
Allocated to Sheffield Freight Terminal. Returned to Capital Stock as a BCV in 1986. Allocated to British Steel, Shelton as 024813 6/88.

041766   B922954   BQV
Allocated to Sheffield Freight Terminal. Returned to Departmental Stock as KDB922954. Scrapped at Coopers Metals, Sheffield 2/91.

041767   B922956   BQV
Allocated to Sheffield Freight Terminal. Scrapped at Roe Bros, Sheffield 2/86.

041768   B922975   BQV
Allocated to Sheffield Freight Terminal. Returned to Capital Stock as a BCV in 1986. Vehicle now stored awaiting disposal at Tyne Yard.

041769   B922995   BQV
Allocated to Sheffield Freight Terminal. Returned to Capital Stock as a BCV in 1986. Scrapped at Booth Roe Metals, Rotherham 8/88.

041770   B923004   BQV
Allocated to Sheffield Freight Terminal. Returned to Capital Stock as a BCV in 1986. Scrapped at Marple and Gillott, Sheffield 4/89.

041771   B923020   BQV
Allocated to Sheffield Freight Terminal. Scrapped at Coopers Metals, Sheffield 12/85.

041772   B923033   BQV
Allocated to Sheffield Freight Terminal. Returned to Capital Stock as a BCV in 1986. Allocated to British Steel, Shelton as 024734 5/87.

041773   B923048   BQV
Allocated to Sheffield Freight Terminal. Scrapped at Coopers Metals, Sheffield 7/91.

041774   B923066   BQV
Allocated to Sheffield Freight Terminal. Scrapped at Coopers Metals, Sheffield 12/85.

041775   B923071   BQV
Allocated to Sheffield Freight Terminal. Returned to Capital Stock as a BCV in 1986. Scrapped at Booth Roe Metals, Rotherham 3/89.

041776   B923075   BQV
Allocated to Sheffield Freight Terminal. Returned to Capital Stock as a BCV in 1986. Scrapped at Coopers Metals, Sheffield 3/90.

041777   B923080   BQV
Allocated to Sheffield Freight Terminal. Scrapped at Coopers Metals, Sheffield 7/91.

041778   B923092   BQV
Allocated to Sheffield Freight Terminal. Scrapped at Coopers Metals, Sheffield 7/91.

041779   B945822   BQV
Allocated to Sheffield Freight Terminal. Returned to Capital Stock as a BCV in 1986. Scrapped at Marple and Gillott, Sheffield 2/89.

041780   B945843   BQV
Allocated to Sheffield Freight Terminal. Returned to Capital Stock as a BCV in 1986. Sold to British Steel, Ravenscraig 8/88.

041781   B945885   BQV
Allocated to Sheffield Freight Terminal. Returned to Departmental Stock as KDB945885. Scrapped at Thomson, Stockton 6/91.

041782   B945903   BQV
Allocated to Sheffield Freight Terminal. Scrapped at Roe Bros, Sheffield 2/86.

041783   B945912   BQV
Allocated to Sheffield Freight Terminal. Returned to Capital Stock as a BCV in 1986. Allocated to British Steel, Shelton as 024736 5/87.

041784   B945940   BQV
Allocated to Sheffield Freight Terminal. Returned to Capital Stock as a BCV in 1986. Sold to British Steel, Ravenscraig 8/88.

041785   -   -
Number issued to B945944 for use at Sheffield Freight Terminal but subsequently cancelled, the vehicle instead being scrapped at Coopers Metals, Handsworth 12/84.

041786   B945946   BQV
Allocated to Sheffield Freight Terminal. Returned to Departmental Stock in 1986 as ADB945946. Scrapped at R&M Supplies, Inverkeithing 4/88.

041787   DB996716   YLO
Allocated to Sheffield Freight Terminal.   Scrapped at Roe Bros, Sheffield 2/86.

041788   DB996731   YLO
Allocated to Sheffield Freight Terminal.   Scrapped at Roe Bros, Sheffield 2/86.

041789   DB996777   YLO
Allocated to Sheffield Freight Terminal.   Scrapped at Coopers Metals, Sheffield 12/85.

041790   DW40053   YLO
Allocated to Sheffield Freight Terminal.   Scrapped at Coopers Metals, Sheffield 12/85.

041791   DW60840   YLO
Allocated to Sheffield Freight Terminal.   Scrapped at Coopers Metals, Sheffield 12/85.

041792   KDB941000   YNO
Allocated to Sheffield Freight Terminal.   Returned to Departmental Stock in 1986. Acquired by the National Railway Museum, York 1/91.

041793   B922583   BCV
Allocated to Sheffield Freight Terminal.   Returned to Capital Stock in 1986. Scrapped at R&M Supplies, Inverkeithing 5/90.

041794   B922651   BHV
Allocated to Sheffield Freight Terminal.   Scrapped at Roe Bros, Sheffield 2/86.

041795   B922667   BHV
Allocated to Sheffield Freight Terminal.   Scrapped at Roe Bros, Sheffield 5/86.

041796   B922675   BCV
Allocated to Sheffield Freight Terminal.   Returned to Capital Stock in 1986. Re-allocated again to Sheffield Freight Terminal as 041892 10/86.

041797   B922719   BQV
Allocated to Sheffield Freight Terminal.   Scrapped at Coopers Metals, Sheffield 1/86.

041798   B922723   BCV
Allocated to Sheffield Freight Terminal.   Returned to Capital Stock in 1986. Scrapped at Thomson, Stockton 6/91.

041799   B922727   BHV
Allocated to Sheffield Freight Terminal.   Scrapped at Roe Bros, Sheffield 2/86.

041800   B922764   BHV
Allocated to Sheffield Freight Terminal.   Scrapped at Roe Bros, Sheffield 2/86.

041801   B922768   BQV
Allocated to Sheffield Freight Terminal.   Scrapped at Coopers Metals, Sheffield 7/91.

041802   B922778   BQV
Allocated to Sheffield Freight Terminal.   Scrapped at Roe Bros, Sheffield 5/86.

041803   B922800   BHV
Allocated to Sheffield Freight Terminal.   Scrapped at Coopers Metals, Sheffield 7/91.

041804   B922891   BCV
Allocated to Sheffield Freight Terminal. Returned to Capital Stock in 1986. Vehicle now in unofficial internal use at British Steel, Lackenby.

041805   B922921   BQV
Allocated to Sheffield Freight Terminal. Scrapped at Roe Bros, Sheffield 5/86.

041806   B922950   BQV
Allocated to Sheffield Freight Terminal. Scrapped at Roe Bros, Sheffield 2/86.

041807   B922978   BQV
Allocated to Sheffield Freight Terminal. Scrapped at Coopers Metals, Sheffield 12/85.

041808   B922979   BQV
Allocated to Sheffield Freight Terminal. Returned to Capital Stock as a BCV in 1986. Scrapped at Booth Roe Metals, Rotherham 8/88.

041809   B922987   BQV
Allocated to Sheffield Freight Terminal. Scrapped at Coopers Metals, Sheffield 12/85.

041810   B923036   BQV
Allocated to Sheffield Freight Terminal. Scrapped at Roe Bros, Sheffield 5/86.

041811   B923050   BCV
Allocated to Sheffield Freight Terminal. Returned to Capital Stock in 1986. Scrapped at Booth Roe Metals, Rotherham 4/89.

041812   B923077   BQV
Allocated to Sheffield Freight Terminal. Returned to Capital Stock as a BCV in 1986. Allocated to British Steel, Shelton as 024814 6/88.

041813   B923093   BCV
Allocated to Sheffield Freight Terminal. Returned to Capital Stock in 1986. Sold to British Steel, Ravenscraig 8/88.

041814   B923098   BQV
Allocated to Sheffield Freight Terminal. Returned to Capital Stock as a BCV in 1986. Scrapped at Coopers Metals, Sheffield 4/89.

041815   B945802   BCV
Allocated to Sheffield Freight Terminal. Returned to Capital Stock in 1986. Scrapped at Coopers Metals, Sheffield 4/89.

041816   B945847   BQV
Allocated to Sheffield Freight Terminal. Scrapped at Coopers Metals, Sheffield 12/85.

041817   B945889   BCV
Allocated to Sheffield Freight Terminal. Returned to Capital Stock in 1986. Scrapped at Marple and Gillott, Sheffield 9/87.

041818   B945916   BCV
Allocated to Sheffield Freight Terminal. Returned to Capital Stock in 1986. Scrapped at Booth Roe Metals, Rotherham 12/88.

041819   -   -
Number issued to B945919 for use at Sheffield Freight Terminal but subsequently cancelled, the vehicle instead being sold to British Steel, Bromford Bridge 1/85.

041820   B945961   BCV
Allocated to Sheffield Freight Terminal. Returned to Capital Stock in 1986. Later LDB945961 at Doncaster Hexthorpe ECD. Scrapped at Coopers Metals, Handsworth 8/92.

041821   DE634319   YAO
Allocated to Sheffield Freight Terminal. Scrapped at Roe Bros, Sheffield 4/86.

041822   -   -
Number issued to DE634343 for use at Sheffield Freight Terminal but subsequently cancelled, the vehicle instead being scrapped at Booth, Rotherham 3/85.

041823   DW100699   YLO
Allocated to Sheffield Freight Terminal. Scrapped at Roe Bros, Sheffield 2/86.

041824   KDB941421   YVO
Allocated to Sheffield Freight Terminal. Scrapped at Roe Bros, Sheffield 5/86.

041825   KDB947004   YSO
Allocated to Sheffield Freight Terminal. Scrapped at Roe Bros, Sheffield 5/86.

041826   B572524   MCV
Allocated to Doncaster Works. Scrapped at Doncaster Works by Lincoln Ferrous Metals, Lincoln 8/89.

041827   B558336   MCV
Allocated to Doncaster Works. Scrapped at Doncaster Works by Higgs, Barnsley 2/90.

041828   -   -
Number issued to B783093 for use at Doncaster Works but subsequently cancelled, the vehicle instead becoming KDB783093. Scrapped at Norton Metals, Trafford Park 1/91.

041829   B922548   BCV
Allocated to Sheffield Freight Terminal. Returned to Capital Stock in 1986. Sold to British Steel, Ravenscraig 8/88.

041830   -   -
Number issued to DB994533 for use at Doncaster Works but subsequently cancelled, the vehicle having already been scrapped.

041832   B954367   CAO
Allocated to York Works. Scrapped at Booth Roe Metals, Rotherham 8/91.

041833   B954467   CAO
Allocated to York Works. Scrapped at Booth Roe Metals, Rotherham 8/91.

041834   DW100700   YLO
Allocated to Sheffield Freight Terminal. Scrapped at Roe Bros, Sheffield 2/86.

041835   M80538   NAV
Allocated to York Clifton CS. Later York WRD. Scrapped at York WRD by Maize Metals, Wednesbury 12/88.

041837   KDB730813   ZDV
Allocated to Norwich Trowse. Scrapped at Norwich Trowse by Miller, Downham Market 11/87.

041838   M94109   NPV
Allocated to York Clifton CS. Sold from York Works to Steamtown, Carnforth 2/89. Subsequently resold to Mangapps Railway Museum, Burnham-on-Crouch.

Cowans Sheldon 6.5 ton manual crane 060976 is seen with accompanying match wagon 060977 at Gloucester Horton Road on 1st July 1990. 060976/7 are due to move to the Swansea Vale Railway Society. Stephen Widdowson

Fuel tank wagon 070882 is pictured at the fuelling point at Exeter on 11th August 1991. Stephen Widdowson

083393 at Redhill was built in 1935 as PMV S2216S. Transfer to the departmental fleet as ADS70140 came in June 1961 with transfer to the internal user fleet taking place in February 1981. This photograph is dated 5th October 1983.   Bob Wallace

Waterloo and City match wagons 083405/6 have been stored at a number of locations including Woking, Hoo Junction and latterly Battersea Wharf. This photograph of 083405 was taken at Hoo Junction on 2nd February 1988.   Bob Wallace

041841   -   -
Number issued to B730876 for use at Wakefield WRD but subsequently cancelled, the vehicle instead being scrapped at Coopers Metals, Sheffield 9/85.

041846   B784709   VMV
Allocated to Doncaster Works, although originally intended for Colchester Stanway OHLM Depot. Scrapped at Doncaster Works by Higgs, Barnsley 2/90.

041847   -   -
Number issued to B784728 for use at Colchester Stanway OHLM Depot but subsequently cancelled, the vehicle instead being scrapped at Booth, Rotherham 7/86.

041848   E18747   SK
Allocated to York Works. Believed scrapped at Booth Roe Metals, Rotherham 11/88.

041849   -   -
Number issued to B732342 for use at Wakefield WRD but subsequently cancelled, the vehicle instead being scrapped at Booth, Rotherham 3/86.

041852   94539   NPV
Allocated to York Works. Scrapped at Booth Roe Metals, Rotherham 11/88.

041853   94592   NPV
Allocated to York Works. Scrapped at Booth Roe Metals, Rotherham 11/88.

041854   94646   NPV
Allocated to York Works. Scrapped at Booth Roe Metals, Rotherham 11/88.

041855   KDB772516   ZRV
Allocated to Darnall WRD. Believed broken up by BR at Darnall WRD during 1990.

041856   KDB755583   ZDV
Initially allocated to Norwich Trowse. Later Doncaster Marshgate. Scrapped at Marple and Gillott, Sheffield 8/87.

041857   KDB755880   ZDV
Initially allocated to Norwich Trowse. Later Doncaster Marshgate. Scrapped at Marple and Gillott, Sheffield 8/87.

041858   KDB854463   ZDV
Initially allocated to Norwich Trowse. Later Doncaster Marshgate. Scrapped at Marple and Gillott, Sheffield 8/87.

041863   -   -
Number issued to B558643 for use at Knottingley TMD but subsequently cancelled, the vehicle instead becoming ADB558643. Allocated to Knottingley TMD as 041985 3/88.

041864   -   -
Number issued to B563107 for use at Knottingley TMD but subsequently cancelled, the vehicle instead becoming ADB563107. Scrapped at Coopers Metals, Sheffield 4/90.

041869   94286   NPV
Allocated to March Station Yard. Sold to Railway Vehicle Preservations at the Great Central Railway 12/90.

041870   94709   NPV
Allocated to March Station Yard. Sold to Railway Vehicle Preservations at the Great Central Railway 12/90.

041880   -   -
Number issued to B261605 for use at Crofton PW Yard but subsequently cancelled, the vehicle instead being scrapped at Booth, Rotherham 7/86.

041883   B948018   BPV
Allocated to Ilford T&RSMD. Returned to Departmental Stock as KDB948018 5/92. Vehicle now located in Tinsley Yard.

041884   B948158   BPV
Allocated to Ilford T&RSMD. Returned to Departmental Stock as KDB948158 5/92. Vehicle now located in Tinsley Yard.

041885   -   -
Number issued to ADB784757 but subsequently cancelled. See 041971.

041886   ADW65643   ZDW
Allocated to March TMD. Sold from March TMD to Moveright International and located at MoDAD Long Marston 9/90.

041887   -   -
Number issued (again) to M31225 but subsequently cancelled. See 041896.

041891   B922578   BCV
Allocated to Sheffield Freight Terminal. Scrapped at Coopers Metals, Sheffield 7/91.

041892   B922675   BCV
Allocated to Sheffield Freight Terminal. Scrapped at Coopers Metals, Sheffield 7/91.

041893   B922715   BCV
Allocated to Sheffield Freight Terminal. Scrapped at Coopers Metals, Sheffield 8/91.

041894   B922864   BCV
Allocated to Sheffield Freight Terminal. Scrapped at Coopers Metals, Sheffield 7/91.

041895   B945824   BCV
Allocated to Sheffield Freight Terminal. Scrapped at Coopers Metals, Sheffield 7/91.

041897   -   -
Number issued to 93828 for use at Gateshead TMD but subsequently cancelled. Allocated to Tinsley TMD as 042126 11/88.

041898   B923408   BEV   (First issue of number)
Allocated to Tinsley TMD. Scrapped at Booth Roe Metals, Rotherham 3/88.

041903   TDB916391   ZSO
Allocated to Blyth Cambois TMD. Scrapped at Blyth Cambois TMD by Bird, Long Marston 2/92.

041924   -   -
Number issued to B935199 for use at British Steel, Lackenby but subsequently cancelled, the vehicle instead being scrapped at Booth Roe Metals, Rotherham 10/88.

041925   -   -
Number issued to ADB999031 for use at Neville Hill T&RSMD but subsequently cancelled, the vehicle instead continuing to work between Neville Hill T&RSMD and Immingham TMD.

041926   -   -
Number issued to B740172 for use at British Steel, Lackenby but subsequently cancelled, the vehicle instead being scrapped at Booth Roe Metals, Rotherham 6/88.

041927   -   -
Number issued to B740205 for use at British Steel, Lackenby but subsequently cancelled, the vehicle instead being scrapped at Coopers Metals, Sheffield 5/89.

041928   -   -
Number issued to B740366 for use at British Steel, Lackenby but subsequently cancelled, the vehicle instead being scrapped at Sheppards, Seaforth 7/87.

041929   -   -
Number issued to B740522 for use at British Steel, Lackenby but subsequently cancelled, the vehicle instead being scrapped at Booth Roe Metals, Rotherham 6/88.

041930   -   -
Number issued to B740619 for use at British Steel, Lackenby but subsequently cancelled, the vehicle instead being scrapped at Booth Roe Metals, Rotherham 11/88.

041931   -   -
Number issued to B740768 for use at British Steel, Lackenby but subsequently cancelled, the vehicle instead being scrapped at Booth Roe Metals, Rotherham 7/88.

041932   -   -
Number issued to B740792 for use at British Steel, Lackenby but subsequently cancelled, the vehicle instead being scrapped at Marple and Gillott, Sheffield 11/88.

041933   -   -
Number issued to B740830 for use at British Steel, Lackenby but subsequently cancelled, the vehicle instead becoming KDB740830. Vehicle now in use in the Newport, Gwent area.

041934   -   -
Number issued to B740842 for use at British Steel, Lackenby but subsequently cancelled, the vehicle instead being scrapped at Sheppards, Seaforth 7/87.

041935   -   -
Number issued to B740943 for use at British Steel, Lackenby but subsequently cancelled, the vehicle instead being scrapped at Sheppards, Seaforth 7/87.

041936   -   -
Number issued to B740963 for use at British Steel, Lackenby but subsequently cancelled, the vehicle instead being scrapped at Booth Roe Metals, Rotherham 6/88.

041937   -   -
Number issued to B740983 for use at British Steel, Lackenby but subsequently cancelled, the vehicle instead being scrapped at Coopers Metals, Handsworth 10/87.

041938   -   -
Number issued to B741038 for use at British Steel, Lackenby but subsequently cancelled, the vehicle instead becoming KDB741038. Vehicle now in use in the Glasgow area.

041939   -   -
Number issued to B741108 for use at British Steel, Lackenby but subsequently cancelled, the vehicle instead being scrapped at Booth Roe Metals, Rotherham 7/88.

041940   -   -
Number issued to B741197 for use at British Steel, Lackenby but subsequently cancelled, the vehicle instead being scrapped at Booth Roe Metals, Rotherham 6/88.

041941   -   -
Number issued to B741306 for use at British Steel, Lackenby but subsequently cancelled, the vehicle instead becoming KDB741306. Vehicle sold to Coopers Metals, Handsworth.

041942   -   -
Number issued to B741387 for use at British Steel, Lackenby but subsequently cancelled, the vehicle instead being scrapped at Booth Roe Metals, Rotherham 6/88.

041943   -   -
Number issued to B741412 for use at British Steel, Lackenby but subsequently cancelled, the vehicle instead being scrapped at Booth Roe Metals, Rotherham 6/88.

041944   -   -
Number issued to B741682 for use at British Steel, Lackenby but subsequently cancelled, the vehicle instead becoming KDB741682. Vehicle now in use in the Newport, Gwent area.

041945   -   -
Number issued to B741791 for use at British Steel, Lackenby but subsequently cancelled, the vehicle instead being scrapped at Marple and Gillott, Sheffield 11/88.

041948   -   -
Number issued to ADB494471 but subsequently cancelled. See 041983.

041949   -   -
Number issued to ADB723542 but subsequently cancelled. See 041984.

041953   -   -
Number issued to B787205 for use at Sunderland South Dock but subsequently cancelled the vehicle instead becoming KDB787205. Vehicle now stored in Carlisle Kingmoor Sorting Sidings.

041956   -   -
Number issued to ADE321075 but subsequently cancelled. See 041977.

041958   -   -
Number issued to DB994056 but subsequently cancelled as previous internal user number allocated already carried. See 041915.

041959   -   -
Number issued to DB994078 but subsequently cancelled as previous internal user number allocated already carried. See 041916.

041962   ADW44013   ZRV
Allocated to Lincoln TMD. Later Doncaster Hexthorpe ECD. Allocated to Derby Etches Park T&RSMD as 024982 4/92.

041965   -   -
Number issued to ADE961880 but subsequently cancelled as previous internal user number allocated already carried. See 041957.

041967   ADW2592   ZRV
Allocated to Stratford TMD (initially as 041341 in 1/77). Scrapped at Coopers Metals, Sheffield 2/91.

041973   80681   NAV
Allocated to Hull Paragon. Scrapped at Hull Hessle Yard by Maize Metals, Wednesbury 12/90.

041974   84507   NAV   (First issue of number)
Although allocated to Hull Paragon this vehicle never left York Up yard. Its internal user number was carried from 11/87 to 2/88 when it reverted to its capital stock number and was sold to the Colne Valley Railway.

041974   84297   NAV   (Second issue of number)
Allocated to Hull Paragon. Scrapped at Hull Hessle Yard by Maize Metals, Wednesbury 12/90.

041975   ADE320154   QQV
Allocated to Cambridge T&RSMD. Sold from Cambridge T&RSMD to the Colne Valley Railway 10/90.

041976   -   -
Number issued to 80527 for use at Ilford T&RSMD but subsequently cancelled, the vehicle instead being scrapped at Booth Roe Metals, Rotherham 12/88.

041980   B935538   SPV
Allocated to Immingham TMD. Scrapped at Coopers Metals, Sheffield 4/89.

041988   ADW2009   ZRV
Allocated to Shirebrook TMD. Sold from Shirebrook TMD to Mangapps Railway Museum, Burnham on Crouch 6/90.

041990   B338017   HUO
Allocated to British Coal, Lynemouth Colliery. Sold from Blyth West Staithes to the Tanfield Railway Preservation Society, Marley Hill 3/88.

041991   B336817   HUO
Allocated to British Coal, Lynemouth Colliery. Sold from Blyth West Staithes to the Tanfield Railway Preservation Society, Marley Hill 3/88.

041992   -   -
Number issued to B947916 but subsequently cancelled as previous internal user number allocated already carried. See 041910.

041993   ADB68231   ZHO
Allocated to Stratford TMD. Sold from Stratford TMD to the East Anglian Railway Museum, Chappel and Wakes, Colne 9/91.

041996   -   -
Number issued to TDW32818 for use at Little Barford Power Station but subsequently cancelled, the vehicle instead being scrapped at Coopers Metals, Sheffield 9/90.

041997   -   -
Number issued to 80509 for use at Neville Hill T&RSMD but subsequently cancelled, the vehicle instead being sold to the Llangollen Steam Railway 6/89.

042001   -   -
Number issued to B334585 for use at Derbyshire Coalite and Chemical, Bolsover but subsequently cancelled, the vehicle instead being scrapped at Coopers Metals, Sheffield 4/89.

042002   -   -
Number issued to B334889 for use at Derbyshire Coalite and Chemical, Bolsover but subsequently cancelled, the vehicle instead being scrapped at Coopers Metals, Sheffield 4/89.

042003   -   -
Number issued to B333715 for use at Derbyshire Coalite and Chemical, Bolsover but subsequently cancelled, the vehicle instead being scrapped at Coopers Metals, Sheffield 4/89.

042004   -   -
Number issued to B334544 for use at Derbyshire Coalite and Chemical, Bolsover but subsequently cancelled, the vehicle instead being scrapped at Coopers Metals, Sheffield 4/89.

042005   -   -
Number issued to B334371 for use at Derbyshire Coalite and Chemical, Bolsover but subsequently cancelled, the vehicle instead being scrapped at Coopers Metals, Sheffield 4/89.

042006   -   -
Number issued to B335367 for use at Derbyshire Coalite and Chemical, Bolsover but subsequently cancelled, the vehicle instead being scrapped at Coopers Metals, Sheffield 4/89.

042007   -   -
Number issued to B333731 for use at Derbyshire Coalite and Chemical, Bolsover but subsequently cancelled, the vehicle instead being scrapped at Coopers Metals, Sheffield 4/89.

042008   -   -
Number issued to B334117 for use at Derbyshire Coalite and Chemical, Bolsover but subsequently cancelled, the vehicle instead being scrapped at Coopers Metals, Sheffield 4/89.

042009   -   -
Number issued to B334169 for use at Derbyshire Coalite and Chemical, Bolsover but subsequently cancelled, the vehicle instead being scrapped at Coopers Metals, Sheffield 4/89.

042010   -   -
Number issued to B337544 for use at Derbyshire Coalite and Chemical, Bolsover but subsequently cancelled, the vehicle instead being scrapped at Coopers Metals, Sheffield 4/89.

042011   -   -
Number issued to B337677 for use at Derbyshire Coalite and Chemical, Bolsover but subsequently cancelled, the vehicle instead being scrapped at Coopers Metals, Sheffield 4/89.

042012   -   -
Number issued to B334224 for use at Derbyshire Coalite and Chemical, Bolsover but subsequently cancelled, the vehicle instead being scrapped at Coopers Metals, Sheffield 4/89.

042013   -   -
Number issued to B335466 for use at Derbyshire Coalite and Chemical, Bolsover but subsequently cancelled, the vehicle instead being scrapped at Coopers Metals, Sheffield 4/89.

042014   -   -
Number issued to B335108 for use at Derbyshire Coalite and Chemical, Bolsover but
subsequently cancelled, the vehicle instead being scrapped at Coopers Metals,
Sheffield 4/89.

042048   -   -
Number issued to B334759 for use at Derbyshire Coalite and Chemical, Bolsover but
subsequently cancelled, the vehicle instead being scrapped at Coopers Metals,
Sheffield 4/89.

042124   35119   BSK
Allocated to Neville Hill T&RSMD. Scrapped at Booth Roe Metals, Rotherham 4/91.

042125   34532   BSK
Allocated to Neville Hill T&RSMD.   Scrapped by Gwent Demolition and Construction,
Margam 1/92.

042127   B745868   FVX
Allocated to Doncaster Belmont Yard. Scrapped at Doncaster Belmont Yard by Howard
and Wheeler, Ecclesfield 3/92.

042132   84125   NAV
Allocated to Heaton T&RSMD. Scrapped at Booth Roe Metals, Rotherham 2/92.

042136   -   -
Number issued to 3094 for use at Bounds Green/Hornsey Up Sidings/Ferme Park but
subsequently cancelled, the vehicle now being stored awaiting disposal at Wembley
CARMD.

042137   -   -
Number issued to 3122 for use at Bounds Green/Hornsey Up Sidings/Ferme Park but
subsequently cancelled, the vehicle now being stored awaiting disposal at Wembley
CARMD.

042138   -   -
Number issued to 5390 for use at Bounds Green/Hornsey Up Sidings/Ferme Park but
subsequently cancelled, the vehicle instead being scrapped at Booth Roe Metals,
Rotherham 2/91.

042139   -   -
Number issued to 94054 for use at Brighton but subsequently cancelled as an 08XXXX
number should have been issued. See 083632.

042140   -   -
Number issued to 94055 for use at Brighton but subsequently cancelled as an 08XXXX
number should have been issued. See 083633.

WESTERN REGION – 06XXXX

Allocated numbers have reached 061217. Vehicles numbered up to 061100 should have their number engraved on a plate attached to the frame. Some vehicles carry their original identity and an internal user numberplate, whilst others do not carry any sign at all of their internal user identity. Various numbering blocks have been issued including 064XXX, 068XXX and 070XXX. To confuse matters further some numbers have been used more than once. Since the end of 1979 a consecutive block of numbers has been used commencing with 060900.

Current Stock

No.	Former Identity	Carkind	Location
060371	B764356	VVV	Radyr Bridge Works Depot
060482	B758542	-	Shrewsbury (Coleham) Engineers Yard
060504	B764377	VVV	Radyr Bridge Works Depot
060772	-	Cartic Ramp	Dagenham Dock Station
060773	-	Cartic Ramp	Parkeston Quay
060782	DE87343	NRV	Radyr Bridge Works Depot
060795	B708560	FAV	Morris Cowley
060911	M726552	SPO	Landore TMD
060913	B901102	XWO	Old Oak Common TMD
060915	B854353	VSV	Swansea Burrows Sidings
060916	ADB854114	ZDV	Radyr Yard - grounded
060917	ADB853993	ZDV	Radyr Yard - grounded
060918	ADB852292	ZDV	Radyr Yard - grounded
060920	B932019	SPO	Cardiff Canton T&RSMD
060921	B930323	SPO	Landore TMD
060933	B771606	VVV	Swansea Burrows Sidings
060935 *	B777064	VVV	British Steel, Llanwern - grounded
060951	DB850878	ZQV	Taunton Fairwater Yard
060954	ADB770692	ZDV	Cardiff Canton T&RSMD
060957	S4606	NIV	British Steel, Trostre
060960	B923669	BEV	Cardiff Canton T&RSMD
060962	B770850	VVV	Newport Docks
060968	DW100839	ZCO	Radyr Yard
060970	B932219	SPV	Old Oak Common TMD
060973 *	ADB909069	YRP	Plymouth Laira T&RSMD
060976	ADW225	ZZO	Gloucester Horton Road
060977	ADB915761	ZSO	Gloucester Horton Road
060980	ADW272	ZZO	Westbury
060981	ADB505997	ZSO	Westbury
060986	ADW224	ZZO	Swindon RCE Stores
060992	DB755860	ZQV	West Ealing
060997	ADW44065	ZRV	Margam LIP - off track
061003	M81163	NAV	Cardiff Canton T&RSMD
061004	B778244	VVV	Ebbw Vale South Sidings
061005	B904509	XLV	Plymouth Tavistock Junction - off track
061006 *	B905109	FRV	Cardiff Canton T&RSMD
061007	ADW44069	ZRV	Radyr Yard
061008	B784676	VWV	Westbury SD
061009	B762374	VVV	Cardiff Canton T&RSMD (carries 060969 in error)
061010	B786594	VVV	Cardiff Canton T&RSMD (carries 061006 in error)
061014	ADS2008	ZZP	St. Blazey WRD
061015	ADB502826	ZSV	St. Blazey WRD
061018	DB769217	ZQV	Radyr Bridge Works Depot

061022	M94710	NPV	Gloucester RCE Yard
061023	ADW226	ZZO	Cardiff Canton T&RSMD
061024	ADB451100	ZSV	Cardiff Canton T&RSMD
061030	ADB904539	ZVO	Bristol Bath Road TMD
061034	W94798	NPV	Bristol Marsh Junction
061045	B783773	VMW	Swansea Burrows Sidings
061048	B854662	VSV	Newport Alexandra Dock Junction
061050 *	ADB704398	ZSV	Swindon RCE Stores
061054	S392	NFV	Par Harbour
061058	ADB977221	QRV	Margam LIP
061060	94139	NPV	Reading TMD
061061	S94135	RFV	Oxford Station
061062	M94374	NPV	Plymouth Laira T&RSMD
061063	S94557	NPV	St. Blazey WRD
061064	M94852	NPV	Plymouth Laira T&RSMD
061065	DB977204	QQV	St. Blazey WRD
061066 *	B745645	FVV	Plymouth Laira T&RSMD
061067	ADW2504	ZRV	Margam LIP
061068	W1324	NNV	Cardiff Canton T&RSMD
061076	E80622	NCV	Cardiff Cathays CWMD (carries 061075 in error)
061077	M94257	NPV	St Blazey WRD
061078	DB996787	YLO	Radyr Yard
061079	DB996799	YLO	Radyr Yard
061081	ADB909054	YVP	Bristol Bath Road TMD
061082	ADB909025	YVP	Bristol Bath Road TMD
061083	ADB900933	YVP	Bristol Bath Road TMD
061084	ADE230952	ZVV	Bristol Bath Road TMD
061085	ADB909010	YVP	Bristol Bath Road TMD
061086	93427	NKV	Cardiff Cathays CWMD
061090	93574	NKV	Cardiff Canton T&RSMD
061091 *	ADB935669	ZDV	Old Oak Common TMD
061092	KDB904146	ZVP	Bristol Bath Road TMD
061093 *	ADB977220	QXV	Cardiff Cathays CWMD
061094	~~DB977254~~ 94241	NPV	Landore TMD
061095	94581	NPV	Landore TMD
061096	KDB975871	QRV	Swindon RCE Stores
061098	B340618	HTV	British Coal, Gwaun-Cae-Garwen
061099	B430138	HTV	British Coal, Gwaun-Cae-Garwen
061100	B430351	HTV	British Coal, Gwaun-Cae-Garwen
061101	B433544	HTV	British Coal, Gwaun-Cae-Garwen
061119	B340021	HTV	British Coal, Onllwyn Washery
061120	B340157	HTV	British Coal, Onllwyn Washery
061121	B340558	HTV	British Coal, Onllwyn Washery
061122	B340747	HTV	British Coal, Onllwyn Washery
061123	B340820	HTV	British Coal, Onllwyn Washery
061124	B340908	HTV	British Coal, Onllwyn Washery
061125	B423800	HTV	British Coal, Onllwyn Washery
061126	B423884	HTV	British Coal, Onllwyn Washery
061127	B425535	HTV	British Coal, Onllwyn Washery
061128	B425575	HTV	British Coal, Onllwyn Washery
061129	B428094	HTV	British Coal, Onllwyn Washery
061130	B428146	HTV	British Coal, Onllwyn Washery
061131	B429434	HTV	British Coal, Onllwyn Washery
061132	B430016	HTV	British Coal, Onllwyn Washery
061133	B431979	HTV	British Coal, Onllwyn Washery
061134	B432556	HTV	British Coal, Onllwyn Washery
061135	B200967	MDO	British Coal, Onllwyn Washery
061136	B201641	MDO	British Coal, Onllwyn Washery
061137	B202057	MDO	British Coal, Onllwyn Washery

061138	B202095	MDO	British Coal, Onllwyn Washery
061139	B202222	MDO	British Coal, Onllwyn Washery
061140	B202448	MDO	British Coal, Onllwyn Washery
061141	B202467	MDO	British Coal, Onllwyn Washery
061142	B280017	MDO	British Coal, Onllwyn Washery
061143	B280639	MDO	British Coal, Onllwyn Washery
061144	B280841	MDO	British Coal, Onllwyn Washery
061145	B280847	MDO	British Coal, Onllwyn Washery
061146	B281054	MDO	British Coal, Onllwyn Washery
061147	B281092	MDO	British Coal, Onllwyn Washery
061148	B281110	MDO	British Coal, Onllwyn Washery
061149	B281118	MDO	British Coal, Onllwyn Washery
061150	B281308	MDO	British Coal, Onllwyn Washery
061151	B281691	MDO	British Coal, Onllwyn Washery
061152	B281868	MDO	British Coal, Onllwyn Washery
061153	B280253	MDO	British Coal, Onllwyn Washery
061154	B282173	MDO	British Coal, Onllwyn Washery
061155	B282639	MDO	British Coal, Onllwyn Washery
061156	B282942	MDO	British Coal, Onllwyn Washery
061157	B282982	MDO	British Coal, Onllwyn Washery
061158	B281378	MDO	British Coal, Onllwyn Washery
061159	B283334	MDO	British Coal, Onllwyn Washery
061160	B290112	MDO	British Coal, Onllwyn Washery
061161	B290235	MDO	British Coal, Onllwyn Washery
061162	B290240	MDO	British Coal, Onllwyn Washery
061163	B290276	MDO	British Coal, Onllwyn Washery
061164	B290318	MDO	British Coal, Onllwyn Washery
061165	B290342	MDO	British Coal, Onllwyn Washery
061166	B290372	MDO	British Coal, Onllwyn Washery
061167	B290397	MDO	British Coal, Onllwyn Washery
061168	B290420	MDO	British Coal, Onllwyn Washery
061169	DB977154	QRV	Bristol East Depot
061170	B281009	MDO	British Coal, Onllwyn Washery
061171	93480	NKV	Reading TMD
061173	93654	NKV	Old Oak Common CARMD
061174	93197	NKV	Old Oak Common CARMD
061175	B202196	MDO	British Coal, Onllwyn Washery
061176	B281921	MDO	British Coal, Onllwyn Washery
061177	B282983	MDO	British Coal, Onllwyn Washery
061178	B428365	HTV	British Coal, Onllwyn Washery
061179	B311288	MDV	British Coal, Coed Bach Disposal Point
061180	B311051	MDV	British Coal, Coed Bach Disposal Point
061181	B313562	MDV	British Coal, Coed Bach Disposal Point
061182	B310738	MDV	British Coal, Coed Bach Disposal Point
061183	B313284	MDV	British Coal, Coed Bach Disposal Point
061184	B314863	MDV	British Coal, Coed Bach Disposal Point
061185	93921	NKV	Bristol Marsh Junction
061188	DB986252	ZBO	Radyr Yard
061190 *	93190	NKV	Reading Triangle Sidings
061191 *	ADB749652	ZRR	Bristol East Depot
061194	200248	VBA	Margam WRD
061195	200309	VBA	Margam WRD
061196	ESSO66127	TTA	Cardiff Canton T&RSMD
061197	ESSO66132	TTA	Cardiff Canton T&RSMD
061198	ESSO66153	TTA	Margam LIP
061199	ESSO66113	TTA	Landore TMD
061200 *	ESSO66324	TTA	Bristol Bath Road TMD
061201 *	DB994445	YBA	Westerleigh CE Training School
061202	93498	NJV	Plymouth Laira T&RSMD - grounded
061203	93887	NJV	Plymouth Laira T&RSMD

061224 - 228 - 229 CARDIFF CANTON
061223 OXFORD STA.

No.		Former Identity	Carkind	Location
061204	*	93927	NJV	Plymouth Laira T&RSMD
061205	*	KDB977556	QRV	Reading S&T Sidings
061206		KDB977557	QRV	Bristol Kingsland Road
061207		KDB977558	QRV	Bristol Kingsland Road
061208		93776	NKV	St. Blazey WRD
061209	*	DB999045	ZRF	Meldon Quarry
061210		ADB977080	QQV	Westbury SD
061211		ADB506729	ZVV	Margam WRD
061212	*	200212	VBA	Margam WRD
061213	*	200217	VBA	Margam WRD
061214		DB994771	YBA	Cardiff Cathays CWMD
061215	*	200266	VBA	Margam WRD
061216		80559	NDV	Old Oak Common TMD
061217	*	93129	NKV	Old Oak Common TMD
064457		−	−	Aberystwyth
064594		−	−	Aberystwyth
064778		M176216	−	British Steel, Margam
064850		−	−	Pantyffynon − grounded
064864		DE296976	ZGV	Cardiff Canton T&RSMD
068725		DW150365	QRV	Radyr Bridge Works Depot
070830		B755282	VVV	British Steel, Margam
070837		DW300	ZPO	Honeybourne Tip
070838		B710019	FAV	Bridgewater
070840		ADW5	ZRO	Landore TMD
070847		ADW80990	ZRV	Landore TMD
070852		B506170	FAV	Morris Cowley
070855		B851034	VSV	Radyr Bridge Works Depot
070856		B506454	FAV	Morris Cowley
070857		TDB854239	ZDV	Newport Docks
070863		B944769	BCO	Taunton Engineers Yard
070865		B772351	VVV	Landore TMD
070881		DB852276	ZDV	Radyr Bridge Works Depot
070882		ADW150141	ZRV	Exeter FP
070887		B757177	VVV	British Steel, Margam

Vehicles No Longer In Stock

    No.   Former Identity   Carkind

060900   TDB975175   QRV
Allocated to Newbury. Scrapped at Cashmore, Great Bridge 11/84.

060901   ADB763482   ZRV
Allocated to Newbury. Scrapped at Newbury by Reliance Scrap Metals, Parkstone, Poole 2/91.

060902   KDW9899   QPV
Allocated to Westbourne Park. Scrapped at Bird, Long Marston 10/82.

060903   KDW150205   QPV
Allocated to Westbourne Park. Sold to the Great Western Society and based on the Severn Valley Railway 7/82.

060904   KDW9875   QPV
Initially allocated to St. Austell. Transfered to Exeter (Red Cow Crossing) 1982. Sold to the Bodmin and Wenford Railway 2/90.

68

060905   KDW9876   QPV
Initially allocated to St. Austell. Transfered to Exeter (Red Cow Crossing) 1982. Sold to the Bodmin and Wenford Railway 2/90.

060906   KDW9921   QPV
Initially allocated to St. Austell. Badly damaged by fire 1982. Subsequently stored at Exeter Riverside Yard. Scrapped at Marple and Gillott, Sheffield 3/85.

060907   KDW150206   QPV
Initially allocated to St. Austell. Transfered to Exeter (Red Cow Crossing) 1982. Sold to the Blackland Railway 6/89.

060908   ADW17399   ZTP
Allocated to Cardiff Canton T&RSMD. Sold to the Swansea Vale Railway Preservation Society, Six Pit Junction 5/83.

060909   B479631   OHV
Allocated to Acton. Scrapped at Acton by Morris, Romford 2/84.

060910   M496022   SPO
Allocated to Milford Haven. Scrapped at Milford Haven by Williams, Llanelli 3/84.

060912   PDB460078   ZSV
Allocated to Fishguard Harbour. Scrapped at Fishguard Harbour by Two Three Ltd, Gorseinon 2/83.

060914   B763330   VVV
Allocated to Melksham. Scrapped at Woodham, Barry 7/84.

060919   ADW150217   QPV
Initially allocated to Radyr. Later Pantyffynon. Scrapped at Pantyffynon by Williams, Newport 12/87.

060922   E276114   OWV
Allocated to Swindon Works. Scrapped at Swindon Works during 1986.

060923   B478782   OWV
Allocated to Swindon Works. Scrapped at Swindon Works during 1986.

060924   B492519   OWV
Allocated to Swindon Works. Scrapped at Swindon Works during 1986.

060925   B479013   OWV
Allocated to Swindon Works. Scrapped at Swindon Works during 1986.

060926   -   -
Number not issued.

060927   -   -
Number not issued.

060928   B484014   OWV
Allocated to Swindon Works. Scrapped at Swindon Works during 1986.

060929   B477229   OWV
Allocated to Swindon Works. Scrapped at Swindon Works during 1986.

060930   B932111   SPO
Allocated to Swansea Docks. Scrapped at Swansea Docks by Williams, Llanelli 12/87.

060931   ADE70574   ZRV
Allocated to Cardiff Cathays CWMD. Scrapped at Woodham, Barry 10/82.

060932   ADB765533   ZQV
Allocated to Landore TMD. Scrapped at Woodham, Barry 2/83.

060934   B931230   SPO
Allocated to Milford Haven. Scrapped at Milford Haven by Williams, Llanelli 3/84.

060936   ADW44029   ZRV
Allocated to Margam LIP. Scrapped at Margam by Thomas, Swansea 5/89.

060937   B478403   OWV
Allocated to Swindon Works. Scrapped at Swindon Works during 1986.

060938   B486701   OWV
Allocated to Swindon Works. Scrapped at Swindon Works during 1986.

060939   B494406   OWV
Allocated to Swindon Works. Scrapped at Swindon Works during 1986.

060940   TDW133964   ZRV
Allocated to Landore TMD. Scrapped at Woodham, Barry 2/83.

060941   E312923   OWV
Allocated to Swindon Works. Scrapped at Swindon Works during 1986.

060942   M421072   OWV
Allocated to Swindon Works. Scrapped at Swindon Works during 1986.

060943   B478691   OWV
Allocated to Swindon Works. Scrapped at Swindon Works during 1986.

060944   B483930   OWV
Allocated to Swindon Works. Scrapped at Swindon Works during 1986.

060945   B485363   OWV
Allocated to Swindon Works. Scrapped at Swindon Works during 1986.

060946   B486622   OWV
Allocated to Swindon Works. Scrapped at Swindon Works during 1986.

060947   ADB975166   QRV
Allocated to Oxford. Sold to Gloucestershire and Warwickshire Railway Society 12/83.

060948   ADW43935   ZRO
Allocated to Taunton RCE No. 3 Workshop. Scrapped at Taunton by Cartwright, Bilston 7/85.

060949   ADW43950   ZRO
Allocated to Taunton RCE No. 3 Workshop. Scrapped at Taunton by Cartwright, Bilston 7/85.

060950   E260312   SPO
Allocated to Plymouth Laira T&RSMD. Scrapped at Plymouth Laira T&RSMD by Pearse, Exeter 11/81.

060952   B777704   VVV
Allocated to Swansea Docks. Scrapped at Swansea Docks by Williams, Llanelli 12/87.

060953   B763850   VVV
Allocated to Margam WRD. Scrapped at Margam WRD by Ward, Sheffield 6/85.

060955   ADW1983   ZRV
Initially allocated to Landore TMD. Later Margam LIP. Scrapped at Margam LIP by Thomas Demolition, Swansea 5/89.

060956   ADW150143   ZRV
Initially allocated to Landore TMD. Later Margam LIP. Scrapped at Margam LIP by Thomas Demolition, Swansea 5/89.

060958   B923787   BEV
Allocated to Cardiff Cathays CWMD. Scrapped at Woodham, Barry Dock 10/82.

060959   B923808   BEV
Allocated to Cardiff Cathays CWMD. Scrapped at Woodham, Barry Dock 10/82.

060961   B923862   BEV
Allocated to Swansea Burrows Sidings. Later Margam Yard. Scrapped at Woodham, Barry Dock 11/91.

060963   DW80669   ZCO
Allocated to Taunton Fairwater PAD. Sold to the 813 Society 2/89.

060964   ADW44034   ZRV
Allocated to Cardiff Cathays CWMD. Scrapped at Woodham, Barry Dock 10/82.

060965   B478206   OWV
Allocated to work Ebbw Junction - Maesglas Tip. Scrapped at Ashford Works 12/83.

060966   B493981   OWV
Allocated to work Ebbw Junction - Maesglas Tip. Scrapped at Ashford Works 12/83.

060967   DW40340   ZCO
Allocated to Radyr. Sold to Moveright International 7/89.

060969   TDB975201   QXV
Allocated to Cardiff Canton T&RSMD. Scrapped at Cardiff Canton T&RSMD by Knill, Barry 12/82.

060971   TDB975342   QRV
Allocated to Gloucester New Yard. Scrapped at Woodham, Barry 4/83.

060972   TDB975345   QRV
Allocated to Westbury. Sold to the Swindon and Cricklade Railway 9/84.

060974   ADW448   ZZO
Allocated to Swindon Spike Yard. Scrapped at Swindon Spike Yard by Round, Wednesbury 8/82.

060975   ADB735877   ZSV
Allocated to work with 060974 at Swindon Spike Yard. Scrapped at Swindon Spike Yard by Round, Wednesbury 8/82.

060978   ADW550   ZZO
Allocated to Gloucester New Yard. Scrapped at Gloucester New Yard by Round, Wednesbury 8/82.

Latterly an instruction coach for the London Fire Brigade 083409 is seen on 18th August 1991 at Stewarts Lane T&RSMD awaiting collection by a private purchaser. Following the cancellation by BR of that sale a successful bid has been made by the Bluebell Railway.   Brian Cuttell

Rail-carrying wagon 083501 at Ashford PAD on 9th July 1983.   Bob Wallace

Refuse Wagon 083530 is pictured at Hoo Junction on 22nd February 1987 whilst en route from Victoria CS to Car Fragmentation, Ridham Dock. Bob Wallace

095011 is pictured at Ayr TMD on 3rd July 1992. John Godfrey

060979   ADW150471   ZSO
Allocated to work with 060978 at Gloucester New Yard. Scrapped at Gloucester New Yard by Round, Wednesbury 8/82.

060982   ADW446   ZZO
Allocated to Pilning. Sold from Bristol Marsh Junction to the 813 Society 11/83.

060983   ADB707261   ZSV
Allocated to Pilning. Sold from Bristol Marsh Junction to the 813 Society 11/83.

060984   ADS70007   ZZO
Allocated to Bristol Marsh Junction. Scrapped at Bristol Marsh Junction by Round, Wednesbury 8/82.

060985   ADB505649   ZSV
Allocated to work with 060984 at Bristol Marsh Junction. Scrapped at Bristol Marsh Junction by Round, Wednesbury 8/82.

060987   ADE292701   ZSO
Allocated to work with 060986 within the Bristol area. Sold from Bristol Marsh Junction to the Avon Valley Railway 8/83.

060988   ADW340   ZZO
Allocated to Worcester. Sold from Worcester to the Dean Forest Railway 7/82.

060989   ADW150463   ZSO
Allocated to work with 060988 at Worcester. Sold from Worcester to the Dean Forest Railway 7/82.

060990   ADW252   ZZO
Allocated to Bristol Marsh Junction. Scrapped at Bristol Marsh Junction by Knill, Barry 7/82.

060991   ADB451392   ZSV
Allocated to Bristol Marsh Junction. Frame retained for use in 061050, remainder scrapped at Bristol Marsh Junction by Knill, Barry 7/82.

060993   DB770505   ZDV
Allocated to Reading RCE Yard. Scrapped at Woodham, Barry Dock 5/89.

060994   DB776004   ZDV
Allocated to Reading RCE Yard. Scrapped at Reading by Ward Ferrous Metals, Chepstow 6/88.

060995   DB786113   ZQV
Allocated to Reading RCE Yard. Scrapped at Reading by Ward Ferrous Metals, Chepstow 6/88.

060996   ADW146151   ZRV
Allocated to Stoke Gifford. Broken up at Stoke Gifford by BR staff 12/83.

060998   ADW43992   ZRO
Allocated to Old Oak Common TMD. Scrapped at Woodham, Barry Dock 12/82.

060999   ADW44542   ZRV
Allocated to Old Oak Common TMD. Scrapped at Old Oak Common TMD by Morris, Romford 12/82.

061000   ADW2958   ZRV
Allocated to Old Oak Common TMD. Scrapped at Old Oak Common TMD by Morris, Romford 12/82.

061001   B786424   VVV
Allocated to Exeter New Yard. Scrapped at Exeter New Yard by MHS Metals, Gloucester 8/86.

061002   KDB997714   ZVO
Allocated to Old Oak Common TMD. Scrapped at Swansea Docks by Bird, Skewen 7/86.

061011   ADW236   ZZO
Allocated to Hereford. Sold from Hereford to the East Lancashire Railway 6/87.

061012   ADB746416   ZSV
Allocated to work with 061011 at Hereford. Sold from Hereford to the East Lancashire Railway 6/87.

061013   B933808   RRV
Allocated to Park Royal. Scrapped at Woodham, Barry Dock 8/87.

061016   ADB931172   ZVO
Allocated to Park Royal. Scrapped at Woodham, Barry Dock 8/87.

061017   M39475   VFV
Allocated to Taunton Engineers Yard. Scrapped at Woodham, Barry Dock 12/85.

061019   DW104839   ZDO
Allocated to Radyr. Scrapped at Woodham, Barry Dock 11/84.

061020   DB851352   ZQV
Allocated to Radyr. Scrapped at Woodham, Barry Dock 2/90.

061021   DW114202   ZQV
Allocated to Radyr. Sold from Radyr to the Great Central Railway 2/89.

061025   W26109   SK
Allocated to Sudbrook. Stored at Severn Tunnel Junction and then Worcester (London Road) Yard. Scrapped at Booth Roe Metals, Rotherham 1/92.

061026   E81307   NAV
Allocated to Swansea Burrows Sidings. Scrapped at Swansea Burrows Sidings by Bird, Skewen 3/87.

061027   M94433   NPV
Allocated to Bristol Marsh Junction. Scrapped at Mayer Parry, Snailwell 7/91.

061028   M31179   NFV
Allocated to Old Oak Common CS. Scrapped at Old Oak Common CS by Morris, Romford 4/86.

061029   M31305   NFV
Allocated to Old Oak Common CS. Scrapped at Old Oak Common CS by Morris, Romford 4/86.

061031   DB458483   ZAO
Allocated to work between Swindon Works and Swindon RCE stores. Scrapped at Swindon Down Yard by Phillips, Llanelli 10/91.

061032   DW150151   QQV
Allocated to Taunton Engineers Yard. Sold from Taunton Engineers Yard to the GWR Museum, Coleford 6/86.

061033   DW2011   ZRV
Allocated to Taunton Fairwater Yard. Scrapped at Bird, Cardiff Docks 5/86.

061035   94510   NPV
Allocated to Bristol Marsh Junction. Scrapped at Bristol Marsh Junction by Trackwork, Doncaster 10/90.

061036   94555   NPV
Allocated to Bristol Marsh Junction. Scrapped at Bristol Marsh Junction by Trackwork, Doncaster 10/90.

061037   DB976002   YVO
Allocated to Taunton Concrete Works. Scrapped at Taunton East Yard by Sheppard (Group), Southampton 3/90.

061038   DB976003   YVO
Allocated to Taunton Concrete Works. Scrapped at Taunton East Yard by Sheppard (Group), Southampton 3/90.

061039   DB976009   YVO
Allocated to Taunton Concrete Works. Scrapped at Taunton East Yard by Sheppard (Group), Southampton 3/90.

061040   B936378   SEV
Allocated to Cardiff Cathays CMWD. Scrapped at Woodham, Barry Dock 11/89.

061041   ADW43949   ZRO
Allocated to Hereford FP. Sold from Hereford to Steam in Hereford Ltd. 7/88.

061042   -   -
Number issued in error to ADB998536 and subsequently cancelled.

061043   DB975337   QPV
Number issued to enable parts to be utilised in constructing broad gauge coaches at Cardiff Cathays CWMD in 1984.

061044   DB975339   QPV
Number issued to enable parts to be utilised in constructing broad gauge coaches at Cardiff Cathays CWMD in 1984.

061046   ADB975784   QRV
Allocated to Plymouth Laira T&RSMD. Scrapped at Plymouth Tavistock Junction by Berry, Leicester 8/89.

061047   ADB975785   QRV
Allocated to Plymouth Laira T&RSMD. Scrapped at Plymouth Tavistock Junction by Berry, Leicester 8/89.

061049   ADB932358   ZVO
Allocated to Park Royal. Scrapped at Woodham, Barry Dock 8/87.

061051   ADB851011   ZQV
Allocated to Reading RCE Yard. Scrapped at Woodham, Barry Dock 5/89.

061052   DW143645   ZGV
Allocated to St. Blazey WRD. Sold from St Blazey WRD to the Wheal Martyn Museum, St. Austell 12/87.

061053   DW123266   ZQV
Allocated to St. Blazey WRD. Sold from St Blazey WRD to the Wheal Martyn Museum, St. Austell 12/87.

061055   DB946054   YNP
Allocated to Westerleigh. Scrapped at Woodham, Barry Dock 5/89.

061056   B743000   OOV
Allocated to St. Blazey WRD. Sold from St Blazey WRD to the Wheal Martyn Museum, St. Austell 12/87.

061057   ADB975843   QRV
Allocated to St Blazey WRD. Sold from St Blazey WRD to the Bodmin and Wenford Railway during 1990.

061059   B950881   CAP
Allocated to Plymouth Laira T&RSMD. Scrapped at Woodham, Barry Dock 7/88.

061069   DB946052   YNP
Allocated to Taunton Concrete Works. Scrapped at Taunton East Yard by Sheppard (Group), Southampton 3/90.

061070   DB946053   YNP
Allocated to Taunton Concrete Works. Scrapped at Taunton East Yard by Sheppard (Group), Southampton 3/90.

061071   DB946056   YNP
Allocated to Taunton Concrete Works. Scrapped at Taunton East Yard by Sheppard (Group), Southampton 3/90.

061072   B784441   VEV
Allocated to Severn Tunnel Junction. Scrapped at Woodham, Barry Dock 5/89.

061073   DB946058   YNP
Allocated to Taunton Concrete Works. Scrapped at Taunton East Yard by Sheppard (Group), Southampton 3/90.

061074   DB946062   YNP
Allocated to Taunton Concrete Works. Scrapped at Taunton East Yard by Sheppard (Group), Southampton 3/90.

061075   DB946063   YNP
Allocated to Taunton Concrete Works. Scrapped at Taunton East Yard by Sheppard (Group), Southampton 3/90.

061080   DB778436   ZRV
Allocated to Taunton Engineers Yard. Sold to the South Devon Railway 6/91.

061087   93250   NKV
Allocated to Radyr Yard. Scrapped at Coopers Metals, Handsworth 5/92.

061088   93661   NKV
Allocated to Radyr Yard. Sold to Booth Roe Metals, Rotherham but only reached Gloucester Barnwood. Resold to and scrapped at Gwent Demolition and Construction, Margam 8/92.

061089   93676   NKV
Allocated to Radyr Yard. Sold to Booth Roe Metals, Rotherham but only reached Gloucester Barnwood. Resold to and scrapped at Gwent Demolition and Construction, Margam 8/92.

061097   DB977070   QRV
Allocated to Swindon Cocklebury Yard. Sold to Woodham, Barry Dock but only reached Radyr Yard. Resold to and scrapped at Coopers Metals, Handsworth 5/92.

061102   -   -
Number issued to DB425118 for use at British Coal, Coed Bach Disposal Point but subsequently cancelled, the vehicle instead being sent from Margam WRD to Woodham, Barry Dock 9/91.

061103   -   -
Number issued to DB432368 for use at British Coal, Coed Bach Disposal Point but subsequently cancelled the vehicle instead being sold from Margam WRD to Powell Duffryn, Maindy 12/90.

061104   B310518   MDV
Allocated to British Coal, Deep Navigation Colliery. Scrapped at Woodham, Barry Dock 4/89.

061105   B310727   MDV
Allocated to British Coal, Deep Navigation Colliery. Scrapped at Woodham, Barry Dock 4/89.

061106   B311270   MDV
Allocated to British Coal, Deep Navigation Colliery. Scrapped at Woodham, Barry Dock 4/89.

061107   B311308   MDV
Allocated to British Coal, Deep Navigation Colliery. Scrapped at Woodham, Barry Dock 4/89.

061108   B311552   MDV
Allocated to British Coal, Deep Navigation Colliery. Scrapped at Woodham, Barry Dock 4/89.

061109   B312101   MDV
Allocated to Britsih Coal, Deep Navigation Colliery. Scrapped at Woodham, Barry Dock 4/89.

061110   B312214   MDV
Allocated to British Coal, Deep Navigation Colliery. Scrapped at Woodham, Barry Dock 4/89.

061111   B312346   MDV
Allocated to British Coal, Deep Navigation Colliery. Scrapped at Woodham, Barry Dock 4/89.

061112   B312418   MDV
Allocated to British Coal, Deep Navigation Colliery. Scrapped at Woodham, Barry Dock 4/89.

061113   B313130   MDV
Allocated to British Coal, Deep Navigation Colliery. Scrapped at Woodham, Barry Dock 4/89.

```
061114          B312843        MDV
Allocated to    British Coal,  Deep Navigation Colliery.    Scrapped at  Woodham, Barry
Dock 4/89.

061115          B314242        MDV
Allocated to    British Coal,  Deep Navigation Colliery.    Scrapped at  Woodham, Barry
Dock 4/89.

061116          B314267        MDV
Allocated to    British Coal,  Deep Navigation Colliery.    Scrapped at  Woodham, Barry
Dock 4/89.

061117          B314514        MDV
Allocated to    British Coal,  Deep Navigation Colliery.    Scrapped at  Woodham, Barry
Dock 4/89.

061118          B314516        MDV
Allocated to    British Coal,  Deep Navigation Colliery.    Scrapped at  Woodham, Barry
Dock 4/89.

061172          DB461114       ZSV
Allocated to Radyr Yard. Scrapped at Coopers Metals, Handsworth 5/92.
```

061186   -   -
Number issued to DB986123 for use at Marylebone but subsequently cancelled, the vehicle instead being scrapped at Coopers Metals, Handsworth 2/91.

061187   -   -
Number issued to B923216 for use at Marylebone but subsequently cancelled, the vehicle instead being scrapped at Woodham, Barry Dock 12/90.

061189   -   -
Number issued to 94139 but subsequently cancelled. See 061060.

061192   -   -
Number issued to 5308 for use at Laira T&RSMD but subsequently cancelled the vehicle instead being scrapped at Booth Roe Metals, Rotherham 3/92.

061193   -   -
Number issued to 17070 for use at Laira T&RSMD but subsequently cancelled the vehicle instead being scrapped at MC Metal Processing, Springburn, Glasgow 8/92.

SOUTHERN REGION – 08XXXX

Allocated numbers have reached 083650. Vehicles numbered up to 083619 should have their number engraved on a plate attached to the frame. The number series began in December 1950 with 080000 and has been used cosecutively ever since, although some numbers have been issued twice.

Current Stock

No.	Former Identity	Carkind	Location
081033 *	DS97	ZSP	BRML Eastleigh
081973	S44656	VVO	Ashford West Yard
082213	B736701	FAV	BRML Eastleigh
082219	M504037	–	BRML Eastleigh
082764	Runner from DS35	QSO	BRML Eastleigh
082949	S2400	NPV	BRML Eastleigh
083029	DW142357	ZQV	MoD Ludgershall
083038	DW146460	ZQV	Fratton Station Yard
083056	E87588	NRV	Portsmouth and Southsea Station (carries 083055 in error)
083155	B852157	VSV	Chart Leacon T&RSMD
083178	DM748903	ZRO	Angerstein Works – grounded
083210	ADM395941	QXV	Fratton Station Yard
083211	ADM395942	QXV	Fratton Station Yard
083212	ADB999018	ZRO	Stewarts Lane T&RSMD – grounded
083214	CDS12969	ZGV	BRML Eastleigh
083215	ADS5529	ZGV	BRML Eastleigh
083228	B853590	VSV	Fratton Station Yard
083239	DM477028	ZAV	Fratton Station Yard
083242	B882580	VBV	Ashford Wheel Shops – grounded
083262	CDS3151	YRV	BRML Eastleigh
083264	S4047	TSO	Gillingham EMU Depot
083265 *	B881879	VBV	Betteshanger Colliery
083266	B882302	VBV	BRML Eastleigh
083268	S1120	NQV	BRML Eastleigh
083285	S1576	NQV	Strawberry Hill EMU Depot
083289	DS59895	ZQV	Weymouth Quay
083303	B882288	VBV	Crawley New Yard
083306	DS64753	YNO	BRML Eastleigh
083307	DS64633	YNO	Ashford PAD
083310	DS64641	YNO	Ashford PAD
083311	DS64632	YNO	Ashford PAD
083312	DS64634	YNO	Ashford PAD
083327	B882126	VBV	Ramsgate EMU Depot
083328	B882536	VBV	Ramsgate EMU Depot
083329	B882523	VBV	Ramsgate EMU Depot
083332	ADS1854	ZZO	Tonbridge West Yard
083335	B785294	VVV	Brighton Lovers Walk EMU Depot
083361	S4588	NIV	Hamworthy Goods Yard
083379	S4598	NIV	BRML Eastleigh
083393	ADS70140	NPV	Redhill
083394	S1638	NPV	Southampton Up Yard
083403	E87280	ZRV	Hoo Junction
083405	B453213	OLV	Battersea Wharf
083406	B453409	OLV	Battersea Wharf
083409	TDS70160	QXV	Stewarts Lane T&RSMD
083416	ADB999015	ZRO	Chart Leacon T&RSMD
083425	ADM3014	YVO	BRML Eastleigh

083427	W105779	–	Tonbridge West Yard – grounded	
083433	S1618	NPV	Strawberry Hill EMU Depot	
083439	S94752	NPV	East Wimbledon EMU Depot	
083441	B924691	BOV	Basingstoke	
083442	B924685	BOV	Basingstoke	
083443	B924577	BOV	Basingstoke	
083444	B924758	BOV	Basingstoke	
083445	B924518	BOV	Basingstoke	
083446	B924504	BOV	Basingstoke	
083447	B924479	BOV	Basingstoke	
083448	B924529	BOV	Basingstoke	
083449	B924735	BOV	Basingstoke	
083450	B924596	BOV	Basingstoke	
083451	B924792	BOV	Basingstoke	
083452	B924678	BOV	Basingstoke	
083453	B924667	BOV	Basingstoke	
083454	B924466	BOV	Basingstoke	
083455	B924495	BOV	Basingstoke	
083456	B924488	BOV	Basingstoke	
083465 *	ADB749046	ZRW	Eastleigh T&RSMD – grounded	
083468	ADB757797	ZRV	Dinton	
083469	S1854	NPV	Fratton Station Yard	
083470	S2097	NPV	Fratton Station Yard	
083471	S1655	NPV	Fratton Station Yard	
083473	ADB452718	OLV	Basingstoke Barton Mill CS	
083474	ADB453433	OLV	Basingstoke Barton Mill CS	
083490	DW139455	ZGV	Redhill	
083503	ADM700710	ZRV	Three Bridges PAD	
083507	CDS1817	ZRV	BRML Eastleigh	
083517	ADB771824	ZRV	Godstone Tip	
083520	ADB998989	ZRO	Stewarts Lane T&RSMD	
083525	ADB853204	ZRV	Ashford CS	
083526	ADS63045	ZRP	Eastleigh T&RSMD	
083531	DB763771	ZRV	Three Bridges PAD	
083549	B948199	BPV	Three Bridges PAD	
083550	B948291	BPV	Three Bridges PAD	
083551	B948349	BPV	Three Bridges PAD	
083559	CDB506414	ZVV	Ashford Crane Shop	
083560	CDB705545	ZVV	Ashford Crane Shop	
083561	ADS57837	YNP	Eastleigh PAD	
083562	ADS57838	YNP	Eastleigh PAD	
083563	ADS57842	YNP	Eastleigh PAD	
083564	CDB999086	ZRV	BRML Eastleigh	
083565	CDB999087	ZRV	BRML Eastleigh	
083566	CDB998959	ZRV	BRML Eastleigh	
083567	ADB854998	ZRV	Chart Leacon T&RSMD	
083568	ADB905073	XLV	Ashford Crane Shop	
083572	S219	NFV	Slade Green T&RSMD – grounded	
083575	ESSO45096	TSV	Three Bridges PAD	
083576	ESSO45178	TSV	Perth WRD	
083577	ESSO45188	TSV	Perth WRD	
083578	ESSO45258	TSV	Perth WRD	
083580	ESSO45255	TSV	Southampton Up Yard	
083586	CDB701139	ZVV	BRML Eastleigh	
083587	CDB709048	ZVV	BRML Eastleigh	
083588	CDB709596	ZVV	BRML Eastleigh	
083589	CDB709484	ZVV	BRML Eastleigh	
083592	M94199	NPV	BRML Eastleigh	
083593	M94351	NPV	BRML Eastleigh	
083594	M94762	NPV	BRML Eastleigh	

No.	Former Identity	Carkind	Location
083596	S242	NFV	BRML Eastleigh
083598	ADB999088	ZRF	Bournemouth EMU Depot
083599 *	ADB999089	ZRF	Stewarts Lane T&RSMD
083600	ADB999090	ZRF	Ramsgate EMU Depot
083601	ADB882635	ZRV	Faversham
083602 *	M94494	NPV	Three Bridges Station
083603	84128	NAV	East Wimbledon EMU Depot - grounded
083604	80740	NAV	Selhurst T&RSMD
083607	ADS70129	QPV	Selhurst T&RSMD
083608	ADS70020	QRV	BRML Eastleigh
083610	ADB975889	QRV	Strawberry Hill EMU Depot
083611 *	ADB975890	QRV	Strawberry Hill EMU Depot - grounded
083613	ADB977067	QRV	Strawberry Hill EMU Depot
083614	S99608	NYV	Cardiff Cathays CWMD
083615 *	S255	NFV	Chart Leacon T&RSMD - grounded
083618 *	S210	NFV	Eastleigh T&RSMD
083619	ADB740276	ZDV	Faversham
083620 *	ADE260859	ZVV	Stewarts Lane T&RSMD
083621	ADS70320	QXV	Ashford West Yard
083622 *	BP064686	TTF	Hoo Junction
083623 *	BP064375	TTF	Hoo Junction
083624 *	BP064465	TTF	Hoo Junction
083625	ADM723266	ZSP	Ashford Crane Shop
083626	ADM725605	ZSP	Ashford Crane Shop
083627 *	ADS39617	ZDW	Selhurst T&RSMD
083629	DB994449	YBP	Tattenham Corner
083630	DB900012	ZVR	Tattenham Corner
083631	B902612	RFQ	Selhurst T&RSMD
083632	94054	NMV	Brighton Lovers Walk EMU Depot
083633	94055	NMV	Brighton Lovers Walk EMU Depot
083636	99200	NWX	Strawberry Hill EMU Depot
083637	99203	NWX	Strawberry Hill EMU Depot
083639 *	ADB900600	YVR	Eastleigh T&RSMD
083640	DB985824	ZBV	Hoo Junction
083641	ADS70251	QXW	Chart Leacon T&RSMD
083642 *	DB994107	YBO	Stewarts Lane T&RSMD
083643 *	KDB778561	ZRV	Stewarts Lane T&RSMD
083644	ADB889201	YRX	Eastleigh T&RSMD
083645	ADC200018	ZRA	Eastleigh T&RSMD
083646	ADC200123	ZRA	Eastleigh T&RSMD
083647 *	ADB783056	ZXW	Stewarts Lane T&RSMD
083648 *	93611	NJV	Chart Leacon T&RSMD
083649 *	80966	NCV	Chart Leacon T&RSMD
083650 *	93100	NKV	Chart Leacon T&RSMD

083664   083665

Vehicles No Longer In Stock

No.   Former Identity   Carkind

083400   B775051   VVV
Allocated to East Wimbledon EMU Depot. Scrapped at Car Fragmentation, Ridham Dock 6/84.

083401   B764648   VVV
Initially allocated to Coulsdon North. Later Three Bridges. Scrapped at Car Fragmentation, Ridham Dock 2/88.

083402   E87720   NRV
Allocated to East Croydon. Scrapped at Car Fragmentation, Ridham Dock 3/87.

083404   B757226   VVV
Initially allocated to Three Bridges. Later Norwood Junction. Believed broken up by BR at New Cross Gate during 1986/87.

083407   B451227   OLV
Allocated to Eastleigh PAD. Sold to Coopers Metals, Handsworth and moved to Langley Green 2/89. Resold to the Great Central Railway and stored at Toton WRD until the latter part of 1990.

083408   B453115   OLV
Allocated to Eastleigh PAD. Scrapped at Coopers Metals, Handsworth 2/89.

083410   ADS6   QPV
Allocated to New Cross Gate. Scrapped at Car Fragmentation, Ridham Dock 5/88.

083411   DB707338   FAV
Allocated to Redbridge. Scrapped at Redbridge by Shipbreaking, Queenborough 8/90.

083412   DB706602   FAV
Allocated to Redbridge. Scrapped at Redbridge by Shipbreaking, Queenborough 8/90.

083413   B758923   VVV
Allocated to Ashford Works. Scrapped at Ashford Works 5/84.

083414   B774887   VVV
Allocated to Ashford Works. Scrapped at Ashford Works 3/82.

083415   -   -
Number issued to S94326 for use at New Cross Gate but subsequently cancelled. See 083434.

083417   B486343   OWO
Allocated to Ashford Works. Scrapped at Ashford Works 2/84.

083418   B498991   OWO
Allocated to Ashford Works. Scrapped at Ashford Works 4/84.

083419   B493109   OWO
Allocated to Ashford Works. Scrapped at Ashford Works 2/84.

083420   M488529   OHO
Allocated to Ashford Works. Scrapped at Ashford Works 2/84.

083421   B492062   OWO
Allocated to Ashford Works. Scrapped at Ashford Works 2/84.

083422   B494164   OWO
Allocated to Ashford Works. Scrapped at Ashford Works 2/84.

083423   M422376   OWO
Allocated to Ashford Works. Scrapped at Ashford Works 2/84.

083424   DS13159   ZGO
Allocated to Ashford Works. Scrapped at Ashford Works 2/84.

083426   M701061   -
Allocated to Clapham Junction. Broken up at Tonbridge by BR 10/85.

083428   ADS163   QPV
Allocated to New Cross Gate. Scrapped at Car Fragmentation, Ridham Dock 5/88.

083429   B785306   VVV
Allocated to Dinton. Scrapped at Ashford Works 4/84.

083430   B964118   RTA
Allocated to Slade Green T&RSMD. Scrapped at Ashford Works 4/82.

083431   S1987   NPV
Allocated to Wimbledon West Yard. Scrapped at Woodham, Barry Dock 7/88.

083432   S2509   NPV
Allocated to Wimbledon West Yard. Scrapped at Woodham, Barry Dock 7/88.

083434   S94326   NPV
Allocated to Clapham Junction. Scrapped at Car Fragmentation, Ridham Dock 5/88.

083435   KDS12   QRV
Allocated to Wimbledon West Yard. Scrapped at Woodham, Barry Dock 7/88.

083436   KDS9   QRV
Allocated to Wimbledon West Yard. Grounded at Wimbledon West Yard 9/83 and subsequently broken up by BR staff 11/87.

083437   KDS3064   QRV
Allocated to Wimbledon West Yard. Grounded at Wimbledon West Yard 9/83 and subsequently broken up by BR staff 12/86.

083438   S94347   NPV
Allocated to Wimbledon West Yard. Scrapped at Booth Roe Metals, Rotherham 12/88.

083440   TDB749653   ZRR
Allocated to Stewarts Lane T&RSMD. Returned to Departmental Stock as DB749653 10/87.

083457   DB461256   ZAV
Allocated to Redbridge. Scrapped at Coopers Metals, Sheffield 3/91.

083458   DB458157   ZAV
Allocated to Redbridge. Scrapped at Redbridge by Cartwright, Tipton 12/86.

083459   DB458028   ZAV
Allocated to Redbridge. Scrapped at Redbridge by Shipbreaking, Queenborough 8/90.

083460   DB458408   ZAV
Allocated to Redbridge. Scrapped at Redbridge by Shipbreaking, Queenborough 8/90.

083461   DB459569   ZAV
Allocated to Redbridge. Scrapped at Redbridge by Shipbreaking, Queenborough 8/90.

083462   DB459799   ZAV
Allocated to Redbridge. Scrapped at Coopers Metals, Sheffield 4/91.

083463   DB459113   ZAV
Allocated to Redbridge. Scrapped at Coopers Metals, Sheffield 4/91.

083464   -   -
Number issued to ADB998989 but subsequently cancelled. See 083520.

083466   DS64639   YNO
Initially allocated to Ashford PAD. Later Godstone Tip. Scrapped at Godstone Tip by Phillips Metals, Llanelli 3/89.

083467   -   -
Number issued to DS64738 for use at Ashford PAD but subsequently cancelled, the
vehicle instead being scrapped at Ashford Works 11/83.

083472   ADB740053   SOV
Allocated to Guildford. Scrapped at Car Fragmentation, Ridham Dock 5/88.

083475   ADS70139   QRV
Allocated to Eastleigh Dorset Siding. Scrapped at Booth Roe Metals, Rotherham 3/89.

083476   ADB751965   ZRV
Allocated to Eastleigh Dorset Siding. Scrapped at Coopers Metals, Handsworth 3/89.

083477   ADB975671   QPV
Allocated to Eastleigh Dorset Siding. Scrapped at Booth Roe Metals, Rotherham 3/89.

083478   B964120   RTA
Allocated to Slade Green T&RSMD. Scrapped at Ashford Works 12/83.

083479   DB458538   ZAV
Initially allocated to Slade Green T&RSMD. Later Redbridge. Finally Eastleigh PAD.
Scrapped at Coopers Metals, Handsworth 2/89.

083480   DB459931   ZAV
Initially allocated to Slade Green T&RSMD. Later Redbridge. Scrapped at Redbridge
by Cartwright, Tipton 12/86.

083481   DB460001   ZAV
Initially allocated to Slade Green T&RSMD. Later Redbridge. Scrapped at Coopers
Metals, Sheffield 3/91.

083482   DB461216   ZAV
Initially allocated to Slade Green T&RSMD. Later Redbridge. Scrapped at Coopers
Metals, Sheffield 4/91.

083483   DB461041   ZAV
Initially allocated to Three Bridges PAD. Later Redbridge. Scrapped at Redbridge
by Shipbreaking, Queenborough 8/90.

083484   -   -
Number issued to a minfit (no specific vehicle selected) for use at Norwood Junction
but subsequently cancelled.

083485   -   -
Number issued to a minfit (no specific vehicle selected) for use at Norwood Junction
but subsequently cancelled.

083486   -   -
Number issued to a minfit (no specific vehicle selected) for use at Norwood Junction
but subsequently cancelled.

083487   -   -
Number issued to a minfit (no specific vehicle selected) for use at Norwood Junction
but subsequently cancelled.

083488   ADB764480   ZRV
Allocated to Guildford. Later Woking. Scrapped at Coopers Metals, Handsworth 5/92.

083489   ADS48564   ZRV
Allocated to Guildford. Later Woking. Scrapped at Coopers Metals, Handsworth 5/92.

083491   ADB762800   ZRV
Initially allocated to Brighton CED. Later Three Bridges PAD. Scrapped at Three Bridges PAD by Phillips Metals, Llanelli 3/89.

083492   ADS178   QPV
Allocated to Brighton CED. Scrapped at Vic Berry, Leicester 4/90.

083493   ADW142080   ZPO
Allocated to Horsham. Scrapped at Horsham by Goldpawn, Swansea 11/85.

083494   -   -
Number issued to DB763771 for use at Woking, but subsequently cancelled. See 083531.

083495   DB458582   ZAV
Allocated to Slade Green T&RSMD. Transferred to Redbridge 3/84 and renumbered 083545.

083496   DB460710   ZAV
Allocated to Slade Green T&RSMD. Transferred to Redbridge 3/84 and renumbered 083546.

083497   DB459334   ZAV
Allocated to Slade Green T&RSMD. Transferred to Redbridge 3/84 and renumbered 083547.

083498   -   -
Number issued to DB459195 for use at Slade Green T&RSMD but subsequently cancelled, the vehicle instead being scrapped at Ashford Works 3/83.

083499   ADS63044   ZRP
Allocated to Eastleigh PAD. Scrapped at Coopers Metals, Handsworth 2/89.

083500   -   -
Number issued to ADS63045 but subsequently cancelled. See 083526.

083501   CDS57947   YNO
Allocated to Ashford PAD. Scrapped at Car Fragmentation, Ridham Dock 8/87.

083502   CDS57963   YNO
Allocated to Ashford PAD. Scrapped at Car Fragmentation, Ridham Dock 8/87.

083504   CDW2015   ZRO
Allocated to BRML Eastleigh. Scrapped at Eastleigh Field Sidings by Texas Metals, Hyde 11/85.

083505   CDS541   ZRV
Allocated to BRML Eastleigh. Scrapped at Coopers Metals, Handsworth 12/89.

083506   CDS1728   ZRV
Allocated to BRML Eastleigh. Scrapped at Coopers Metals, Handsworth 12/89.

083508   CDS1818   ZRV
Allocated to BRML Eastleigh. Scrapped at Coopers Metals, Handsworth 12/89.

083509   B740883   SOV
Allocated to Stewarts Lane T&RSMD. Sold for further use to RNAD Bedenham 4/87.

083510   DB740625   SOV
Allocated to Stewarts Lane T&RSMD. Sold for further use to RNAD Bedenham 4/87.

083511   DB740232   SOV
Allocated to Stewarts Lane T&RSMD.   Sold for further use to RNAD Bedenham 4/87.

083512   DB741631   SOV
Allocated to Stewarts Lane T&RSMD.   Sold for further use to RNAD Bedenham 4/87.

083513   DB775369   ZRV
Allocated to Norwood Junction. Believed broken up by BR at New Cross Gate during 1986/87.

083514   DB771959   ZRV
Allocated to Norwood Junction. Scrapped at Car Fragmentation, Ridham Dock 8/86.

083515   DB768127   ZRV
Allocated to Norwood Junction. Believed broken up by BR at New Cross Gate during 1986/87.

083516   ADB779852   ZRV
Allocated to Woking. Scrapped at Coopers Metals, Handsworth 5/92.

083518   B783262   VMV
Allocated to Eastleigh. Scrapped at Coopers Metals, Handsworth 4/92.

083519   ADW44050   ZRO
Allocated to St. Leonards. Scrapped at Car Fragmentation, Ridham Dock 9/84.

083521   ADB977039   QRV
Allocated to BRML Eastleigh. Scrapped at Booth Roe Metals, Rotherham 3/89.

083522   ADB977066   QRV
Allocated to BRML Eastleigh. Scrapped at Booth Roe Metals, Rotherham 3/89.

083523   ADB975276   QRV
Allocated to BRML Eastleigh. Sold to Coopers Metals, Handsworth and moved to Langley Green. Resold to Booth Roe Metals and scrapped at Rotherham 2/92.

083524   ADB977077   QRV
Allocated to Clapham Junction. Returned to Departmental Stock as ADB977077 5/84.

083527   ADB975639   QRV
Allocated to Horsham. Returned to Departmental Stock as ADB975639 2/84.

083528   S1561   NFV
Allocated to BRML Eastleigh. Scrapped at Booth Roe Metals, Rotherham 3/89.

083529   -   -
Number issued to DB740719 for use at Stewarts Lane T&RSMD but subsequently cancelled, the vehicle instead being sold for further use to RNAD Bedenham 5/88.

083530   TDB475740   ZGV
Allocated to Victoria CS. Scrapped at Car Fragmentation, Ridham Dock 3/87.

083532   DB457830   ZAV
Allocated to Redbridge. Scrapped at Redbridge by Shipbreaking, Queenborough 8/90.

083533   DB458343   ZAV
Allocated to Redbridge. Scrapped at Coopers Metals, Sheffield 3/91.

083534   DB458700   ZAV
Allocated to Redbridge. Scrapped at Redbridge by Cartwright, Tipton 12/86.

```
083535        DB458762        ZAV
Allocated to Redbridge. Scrapped at Coopers Metals, Sheffield 3/91.

083536        DB459788        ZAV
Allocated to Redbridge. Scrapped at Coopers Metals, Sheffield 4/91.

083537        DB461261        ZAV
Allocated to Redbridge. Scrapped at Redbridge by Cartwright, Tipton 12/86.

083538        DB457647        ZAV
Allocated to Redbridge. Scrapped at Coopers Metals, Sheffield 3/91.

083539        DB461071        ZAV
Allocated to Redbridge. Scrapped at Redbridge by Shipbreaking, Queenborough 8/90.

083540        DB458449        ZAV
Allocated to Redbridge. Scrapped at Redbridge by Shipbreaking, Queenborough 8/90.

083541           -               -
Number issued to DB459829 for use at Redbridge but subsequently cancelled, the
vehicle instead being scrapped at Ashford Works 4/84.

083542        DB460732        ZAV
Allocated to Redbridge. Scrapped at Coopers Metals, Sheffield 3/91.

083543        DB461226        ZAV
Allocated to Redbridge. Scrapped at Coopers Metals, Sheffield 3/91.

083544        DB461596        ZAV
Allocated to Redbridge. Scrapped at Redbridge by Shipbreaking, Queenborough 8/90.

083545         083495         ZAV
Allocated to Redbridge. Scrapped at Redbridge by Shipbreaking, Queenborough 8/90.

083546         083496         ZAV
Allocated to Redbridge. Scrapped at Redbridge by Cartwright, Tipton 12/86.

083547         083497         ZAV
Allocated to Redbridge. Scrapped at Redbridge by Shipbreaking, Queenborough 8/90.

083548        B948173         BPV
Allocated to Three Bridges PAD. Scrapped at Car Fragmentation, Ridham Dock 7/87.

083552        B948353         BPV
Allocated to Three Bridges PAD. Scrapped at Car Fragmentation, Ridham Dock 7/87.

083553        DB460411        ZAV
Allocated to Redbridge. Scrapped at Redbridge by Shipbreaking, Queenborough 8/90.

083554        DB996756        YLO
Allocated to Norwood Junction. Scrapped at Car Fragmentation, Ridham Dock 8/87.

083555        DW40092         YLO
Allocated to Norwood Junction. Scrapped at Car Fragmentation, Ridham Dock 8/87.

083556        DW40059         YLO
Allocated to Norwood Junction. Scrapped at Car Fragmentation, Ridham Dock 8/87.

083557        DW60838         YLO
Allocated to Norwood Junction. Scrapped at Car Fragmentation, Ridham Dock 8/87.
```

083558   -   -
Number issued to a vehicle (no specific vehicle selected) for use at Three Bridges but subsequently cancelled.

083569   S19   LT Coach
Allocated to Sandown (IoW). Grounded 7/86. Scrapped at Sandown by Jolliffe, Newport (IoW) 5/89.

083570   S30   LT Coach
Allocated to Ryde (IoW). Grounded. Scrapped at Ryde by Oxley, Thomas and Associates, Horndon on the Hill during the first part of 1990.

083571   S205   NFV
Allocated to Waterloo. Sold from Hoo Junction to the Tonbridge Model Engineering Society, Brightfriars Meadow, Tonbridge 6/89.

083573   ADB975277   QRV
Allocated to New Cross Gate. Scrapped at Car Fragmentation, Ridham Dock 5/88.

083574   S99607   NYV
Allocated to Salisbury. Scrapped at MC Metal Processing, Springburn, Glasgow 7/91.

083579   ESSO45296   TSV
Allocated to Woking PAD. Transferred to Departmental Stock as DB999097 1/87.

083581   -   -
Number issued to CDB940695 for use at Norwood Junction, but subsequently cancelled. See 083597.

083582   CDB940813   YVW
Allocated to Norwood Junction, although internal user number never carried. Returned to Departmental Stock as DB940813 in 1987.

083583   CDE306504   YVP
Allocated to Norwood Junction although internal user number never carried. Scrapped at Car Fragmentation, Ridham Dock 8/87.

083584   CDW32818   YSW
Allocated to Norwood Junction although internal user never carried. Transferred to Eastern Region in 1987 where it was to become 041996 at Little Barford Power Station. Cancelled and scrapped at Coopers Metals, Sheffield 9/90.

083585   CDW70307   YSW
Allocated to Norwood Junction although internal user number never carried. Returned to Departmental Stock in 1987 as TDW70307, now ADW70307.

083590   CDB940517   YVW
Allocated to Ashford PAD. Scrapped at Car Fragmentation, Ridham Dock 8/87.

083591   ADB453147   OLV
Allocated to Faversham. Broken up at Faversham by BR 10/87.

083595   S213   NFV
Allocated to BRML Eastleigh. Scrapped at Vic Berry, Leicester 7/87.

083597   CDB940695   YVW
Allocated to Brighton. Scrapped at Car Fragmentation, Ridham Dock 8/87.

083605   ADB904041   ZVP
Allocated to Redbridge. Scrapped at Redbridge by Shipbreaking, Queenborough 8/90.

083606   DB460575   ZAV
Allocated to Woking. Sold from Eastleigh to the Kent and East Sussex Railway 7/88.

083609   B740879   SOV
Allocated to Slade Green T&RSMD. Scrapped at Car Fragmentation, Ridham Dock 5/88.

083612   ADB977065   QRV
Allocated to Strawberry Hill EMU Depot. Sold to Booth Roe Metals, Rotherham. Resold to the Swanage Railway 8/90.

083616   84611   NDV
Allocated to Selhurst T&RSMD. Scrapped at Gwent Demolition and Construction, Margam 7/92.

083617   -   -
Number issued to ADS70129 for use at Selhurst, but subsequently cancelled. Instead ADS70129 replaced ADS70130 the vehicle originally intended to become 083607. ADS70130 was scrapped at Marple and Gillott, Sheffield 11/88.

083620   84103   NDV   (Second issue of number)
Allocated to Three Bridges PAD. Scrapped at Gwent Demolition and Construction, Margam 8/92.

083628   TDB932437   ZSR
Allocated to Eastleigh Methanol Sidings. Sold to Pallot Working Steam Museum, Rue de Bechet, Trinity, Jersey, Channel Isles 6/90.

083634   ADB900410   YXQ
Allocated to Eastleigh T&RSMD. Scrapped at Eastleigh T&RSMD by Sheppard (Group), Southampton 5/92.

083635   ADS39555   ZDW   (Carried 083618 in error)
Allocated to Eastleigh Methanol Sidings. Scrapped at Coopers Metals, Handsworth 4/92.

083638   S99601   NYV
Allocated to Salisbury. Scrapped at MC Metal Processing, Springburn, Glasgow 7/91.

SCOTTISH REGION – 09XXXX

Of all the regions the least use of internal users is made by the Scottish Region. Although it had been intended to now only use the 095XXX series, occasional use is still being made of the 096XXX series and the 097XXX series. Allocated numbers have reached 095030, 096061 and 097014.

Current Stock

No.	Former Identity	Carkind	Location
095006	–	VVV	Cadder Yard – grounded
095007	B780368	VVV	Polmadie CARMD
095008	B769267	VVV	Perth CS
095011	B781259	VVV	Ayr TMD – grounded
095012	ADB882517	ZDV	Polmadie CARMD (carries 09512 in error)
095013 *	ADB786095	ZDV	Polmadie CARMD
095014	M31190	NFV	Motherwell TMD – grounded
095016	M31122	NFV	Motherwell TMD
095017	ADB772744	ZDV	Grangemouth SD
095018	ADB778743	ZDV	Grangemouth SD
095019	LDM265246	ZDV	Carstairs OHLM Depot
095020	ADE321109	QQV	Inverness Yard (carries 095022 in error)
095021	ADB531008	YVP	Eastfield TMD
095023	LDM510859	ZYV	Carstairs OHLM Depot
095024 *	DB975210	QPV	Slateford Civil Engineers Yard
095025 *	DB994176	YBQ	Millerhill Yard
095026	KDB769607	ZDV	Perth WRD
095027	KDB763226	ZRV	Perth WRD
095028 *	ADB975078	QQX	Perth CS
095029 *	ADB975478	QPX	Perth CS
095030 *	96140	NXA	Craigentinny T&RSMD
096033 *	TDB752733	ZDV	Wiggins Teape Paper Mill, Corpach
096035	TDM147012	ZRO	Thurso – grounded
096041	TDB748022	ZSV	Stirling Yard
096042	TDB851696	ZSV	Millerhill Yard – grounded (frame only)
096044	B767273	VVV	Inverness Yard
096045	B774704	VVV	Methil Docks – grounded
096047	B784936	VVV	Fort William LIP
096049	B785110	VVV	Inverness Yard
096053	B783686	VMV	Shettleston (en route to Rothesay Dock)
096054	ADB778333	ZDV	Montrose Station
096055	TDE321069	QPV	Perth CS
096056	TDE321070	QPV	Perth CS
096057	TDB786543	ZDV	Grangemouth SD
096058	TDB778627	ZDV	Grangemouth SD
096059	TDB904586	ZSW	Shell Oil Terminal, Bishopbriggs
096060 *	ADE320692	QQV	Perth CS
096061 *	ADB450460	ZVV	Perth WRD
097003	DB761231	ZQO	Rutherglen PW Depot Yard
097005	DB769460	ZDV	Slateford Civil Engineers Yard
097006	DB776718	ZDV	Slateford Civil Engineers Yard
097008	DW60860	YLO	Costain Concrete, Coltness
097009	DB996133	YMO	Rutherglen RCE Training Centre
097014	DB994316	YBA	Polmadie CARMD
099000	M31265	NFV	Perth Engineers Yard

095041 Perth CE YD
095042 ,, ,, ,,
095043 ,, ,, ,,
095044 ,, ,,

Vehicles No Longer In Stock

No.   Former Identity   Carkind

095XXX Series

095000   -   ZRO
Allocated to Eastfield TMD. Sold for further use to P. Stirling, Mossend 12/87.

095001   M31036   NFV
Initially allocated to Cowlairs CS. Later Fort William. Sold from Fort William to the Scottish Railway Preservation Society 5/85.

095002   -   -
Number not issued.

095003   M30972   NFV
Allocated to Cowlairs CS. Scrapped at Cowlairs CS by MC Metal Processing, Springburn, Glasgow 10/91.

095004   ADE320173   QQV
Allocated to Polmadie CARMD. Scrapped at McWilliam, Shettleston 10/80.

095005   B761385   VVV
Allocated to Rutherglen ECD. Believed broken up by BR at Rutherglen ECD during 1984/85.

095009   -   -
Number not issued.

095010   B777956   VVV
Allocated to Falkland Junction. Believed broken up by BR at Falkland Junction during 1985/86.

095015   -   -
Number not issued.

095022   -   -
Number issued to 93358 for use at Perth WRD but subsequently cancelled the vehicle instead being sold to Booth Roe Metals, Rotherham for scrap.

096XXX Series

096000-2   -   -
Numbers not issued.

096003   TDB87121   -
Allocated to Stranraer. Scrapped at Stranraer by Halliday, Stranraer 12/82.

096004   TDE75460   -
Allocated to Stranraer. Scrapped at Stranraer by Halliday, Stranraer 12/82.

096005-10   -   -
Numbers not issued.

096011   TDM396004   QRV
Initially allocated to Coupar Angus. Later Perth. Scrapped at Perth by McWilliam, Shettleston 11/86.

096012   TDM396002   QRV
Allocated to Perth. Scrapped at Perth by McWilliam, Shettleston 11/86.

096013   TDM396005   QRV
Allocated to Coupar Angus. Believed scrapped at Coupar Angus during 1979.

096014-28   -   -
Numbers not issued.

096029   TDS65795   ZDO
Allocated to Wiggins Teape Paper Mill, Corpach. Scrapped at Fort William by Cartwright, Bilston 6/85.

096030   TDM153705   ZRO
Allocated to Oban. Carried the number 096032 in error. Scrapped at McWilliam, Shettleston 2/86.

096031   -   -
Number not issued.

096032   TDB750675   ZDO
Allocated to Wiggins Teape Paper Mill, Corpach. Scrapped at Fort William by Cartwright, Bilston 6/85.

096034   TDM120434   ZRO
Allocated to Thurso. Scrapped at Thurso by Heath, Thurso 5/83.

096036   TDM395944   QRV
Allocated to Kilmarnock. Scrapped at Kilmarnock by McWilliam, Shettleston 3/79.

096037   -   -
Number not issued.

096038   B748478   FVV
Allocated to Paisley Canal. Later Shieldhall. Scrapped at Shieldhall by Macaloney, Coatbridge 3/87.

096039   W130   NFV
Allocated to Thurso. Broken up by BR at Thurso 7/85.

096040   TDB975093   ZSV
Allocated to Shieldhall. Scrapped at Shieldhall by Macaloney, Coatbridge 3/87.

096043   B745681   FVV
Allocated to Paisley Canal. Scrapped at Arnott Young, Dalmuir 2/80.

096046   -   -
Number not issued.

096048   ADB760258   ZDV
Allocated to Paisley St. James. Believed broken up by BR at Paisley St. James during 1984/85.

096050   -   -
Number issued to B771376 for use at Inverness but subsequently cancelled. Scrapped at McWilliam, Shettleston 2/81.

096051   B775175   VVV
Allocated to Leith Docks. Scrapped at Cohen, Wishaw 8/85.

096052   ADB778373   ZDV
Allocated to Leith Docks. Scrapped at Cohen, Wishaw 8/85.

097XXX Series

097001   -   -
Number not issued.

097002   DE166308   ZRO
Allocated to Wick. Believed broken up by BR at Wick during 1984/85.

097004   DE321053   QPV
Allocated to Perth Engineers Yard. Scrapped at White, Inverkeithing 4/85.

097007   DW40093   YLO
Allocated to Costain Concrete, Coltness. Scrapped at R&M Supplies, Inverkeithing 9/89.

097010   DB779952   ZDV
Allocated to Inverness. Sold to MC Metal Processing, Springburn, Glasgow in 1988. Sale cancelled following a shunting accident at Inverness. Scrapped at Inverness by H. Barclay, Inverness 2/89.

097011   DB502855   ZSV
Allocated to Dalmeny and coupled to diesel-electric crane DRF81203. Scrapped at Dalmeny by A-Z Mechanical Engineers, Doncaster 7/90.

097012   DB710134   ZSV
Allocated to Dalmeny and coupled to diesel-electric crane DRF81203. Scrapped at Dalmeny by A-Z Mechanical Engineers, Doncaster 7/90.

097013   DB907226   YVO
Allocated to Costain Concrete, Coltness. Scrapped at R&M Supplies, Inverkeithing 9/89.

099XXX Series

099001   M31213   NFV
Allocated to Inverness CS. Scrapped at McWilliam, Shettleston 7/81.

099001   KDB760365   ZDV   (Second use of number)
Allocated to Irvine S&T Yard. Sold to James Caldwell, Irvine 4/89, the underframe and wheels then being scrapped and the body resold for further use.

099002   KDB778493   ZDV
Allocated to Irvine S&T Yard. Sold to James Caldwell, Irvine 4/89. Resold to the Scottish Industrial Railway Centre, Dalmellington 5/89.

099003   KDB766042   ZDV
Allocated to Irvine S&T Yard. Sold to James Caldwell, Irvine 4/89. Resold to the Scottish Industrial Railway Centre, Dalmellington 5/89.

099004   KDB775806   ZDV
Allocated to Irvine S&T Yard. Sold to James Caldwell, Irvine 4/89, the underframe and wheels then being scrapped and the body resold for further use.

099005   KDB775872   ZDV
Allocated to Irvine S&T Yard. Sold to James Caldwell, Irvine 4/89, the underframe and wheels then being scrapped and the body resold for further use.

099006   KDB769826   ZDV
Allocated to Irvine S&T Yard. Sold to James Caldwell, Irvine 4/89. Resold to the
Scottish Industrial Railway Centre, Dalmellington 5/89.

099007   KDM508660   ZQV
Allocated to Irvine S&T Yard. Sold to James Caldwell, Irvine 4/89, the underframe
and wheels then being scrapped and the body resold for further use.

The internal user fleet is always of interest to anyone interested in preserving vintage rolling stock. This photograph shows 095019 at Carstairs OHLM Depot on 22nd July 1990.
                                                                          Brian Cuttell

Also Available from South Coast Transport Publishing

BRITISH RAIL WAGON FLEET
AIR BRAKED FREIGHT STOCK - No.'s 100000 - 999999
@ £6.95

BRITISH RAIL WAGON FLEET
VOLUME 4 - BRAKE VANS
@ £3.30

BRITISH RAIL WAGON FLEET
VOLUME 5 - ENGINEERS FLEET
@ £5.25

R.I.V. WAGON FLEET
@ £5.95

These publications and further copies of British Rail Internal Users @ £7.95 per copy (all prices inc. post & packing may be obtained from our Mail Order Dept. at the address below:-

33, Porchester Road,
Woolston,
Southampton,
Hampshire SO2 7JB

Please make cheques and postal orders payable to S.C.T. Publishing

Trade enquiries are welcomed and these should be sent to:-

3, Morley Drive,
Bishop's Waltham,
Hampshire SO3 1RX

* * * * * * * * *

COVER PHOTOGRAPHS

Front:-

024507, pictured at Machynlleth on 5th July 1990, is a combination of plate wagon B932593 and an effluent storage tank.   Bob Cole

Rear (Upper):-

Purpose built Civil Engineers saloon DM45030 is pictured at Hereford on 5th May 1991. DM45030 is to be taken into the internal user fleet at York WRD and will be renumbered 042205.   Stephen Widdowson

Rear (Lower):-

The temporary loan in June 1992 of 024995/96 from the Central Ammunition Depot at Kineton to the MoDAD at Ludgershall gave a very rare opportunity for both MkII coaches to be photographed. Painted in Army Green livery and still carrying their capital stock numbers 5421 and 5273, 024995/6 were photographed at Andover in the company of 37009 on 15th June 1992.   Mike Bennett